THE SOUTHERN WAY

CONTENTS

© Kevin Robertson (Noodle Books) and the various contributors 2009
ISBN 978-1-906419-18-9
First published in 2009 by Kevin Robertson
under the **NOODLE BOOKS** imprint
PO Box 279
Corhampton
SOUTHAMPTON
SO32 3ZX
www.noodlebooks.co.uk
Printed in England by
Ian Allan Printing Ltd
Hersham, Surrey

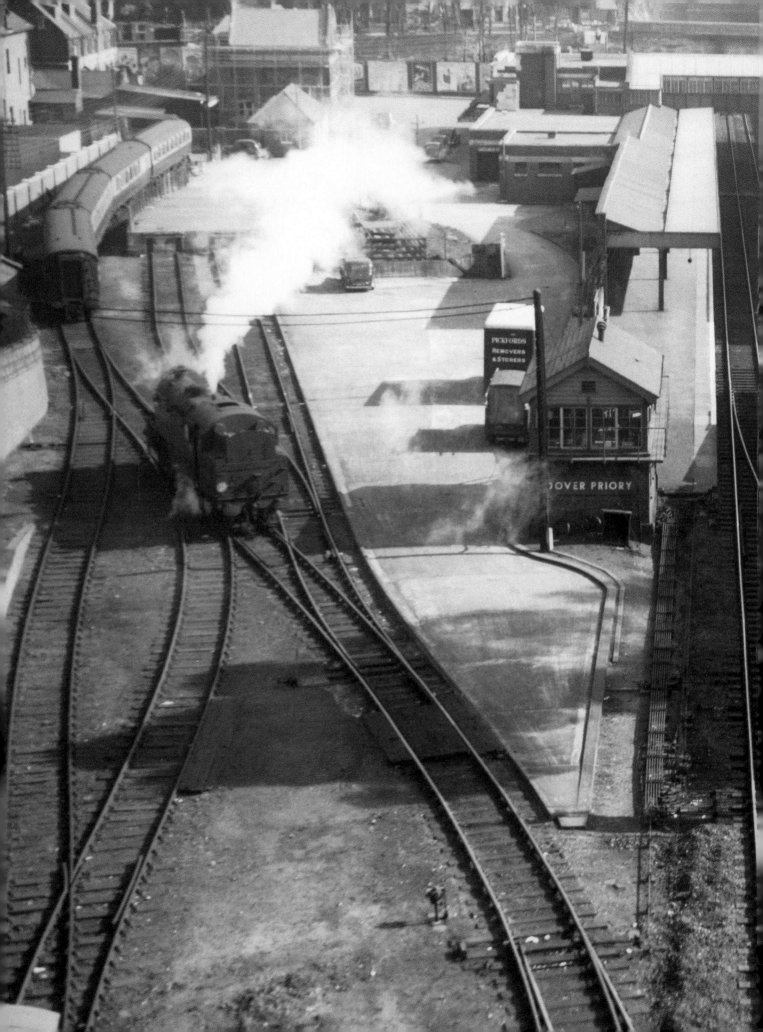

Of all the things I am asked to include in 'Southern Way' that of goods yard scenes ranks amongst the most often requested. Indeed, pick up most books relative to route or branch line histories and there will be a distinct lack of such views, unless shown in the background to something else. The opportunity then to include this view from the West Sussex Past Pictures website (www.westsussexpast.org) was most welcome. The view depicts boring equipment destined for the military being loaded into an LBSCR covered van at Littlehampton sometime during WW1. The goods were stated to be from the local firm of Duke and Ockenden who manufactured pumps and water equipment. The vehicle, No 8100, was of 8 tons carrying capacity and would appear to be in far from pristine external condition as well as giving some indication of recent past loads chalked on to the sides.

Amberley Working Museum Ref: PP/AMCPM/P417

Editorial Introduction

No doubt because of the increased frequency of 'SW' there has been a welcome increase in comments and as someone once so succinctly put it, 'matters arising'. With due deference to the BBC, I suppose we might have been better served by addressing 'Rebuilding' as 'Any Answers', but copyright is a bad enough issue when it comes to the use of photographic images and I have no wish to incur the wrath of an irate broadcaster. That said, please keep your comments coming. There is clearly a wealth of knowledge out there which is indeed humbling to receive and I know I am not alone in welcoming updates and corrections.

I am often asked what are the plans for 'SW', how many issues will there be etc? Dealing with the latter first, a simple response, as many as you are prepared to support, both as regards interest and equally content. With regard to the latter I am delighted to report that material still keeps arriving. Please, do not feel just because you may not have a collection of views or box of information that it cannot be of interest, a single view might well have just the same amount of appeal, whether in colour or b/w - as witness that on page 83 of this issue. Despite then my comment that material keeps arriving, do please help maintain that theme, not just for my sake but for all of us of like interest.

Answering also the question as to what is planned, well I must apologise for the delay in featuring the second part of Lancing, more on Basingstoke, and further selections from Hugh Abbinnett and Norman Denty to name but a few. Space is the simple governing factor. Indeed I had promised Hugh that his 'Small Loco Sheds' article would feature in this issue; then more

arrived for two existing articles and I was instead placed in the obvious dilemma. I promise January for both Lancing Part 2 and Mr Abbinnett. For the future, and leaving aside the obvious continuation of existing series, there are features planned on the Fovant Military Railway - lots of unseen WW1 period views, the C2 and C2X classes, more from Alan Postlethwaite, more on Brighton Works, loco repair details from Ashford, Kent Coast Floods, Southern Diesel-Shunters, Southern Electric Locos and those are the just the ones I can recall at this time. We also have a number of new images from the press agencies and various libraries ready to incorporate as well as several accident features.

I have to perhaps also use this editorial for a slight apology if the promised timescales for certain of our projected books also slip slightly. Judi, Bruce, Peter, Alastair, and the rest of team who all contribute in one way or another are all doing our best, but we have still not found a way of squeezing more hours into the day. The regular issues of 'SW' will continue to be the priority though.

By the time you read this, the new catalogue for 2010 will also be available, probably enclosed with this issue. Two 'Specials' are also in the pipeline, so hopefully a bit of interest there as well.

If we get it wrong, I apologise. If we are a bit late sometimes, I am sorry. So far as the latter is concerned, all I can say is I am only copying the railway and incorporating a recovery margin into the schedule so that a week or so late is still 'on-time' - really!

Kevin Robertson

Previous page: *From the unusual angle of the tunnel above the north end of Dover Priory, Colin Garratt recorded this view looking down upon a busy scene during the early 1950s. To the right the sidings had once formed part of the Engine House and Carriage Shed, although the latter became 'open-plan' consequent upon rebuilding in 1932. The engine facilities had similarly been transferred to a modern depot adjoining the 'Town' station in 1928. The engine departing is No 42095, a Fairburn 2-6-4T whilst two other engines, another 2-6-4T and an 'R1' are similarly employed.*

Corbis IL003194

Front cover: *To accompany our first piece on Oakley, this is the station seen from the cab of a WR type DMU although clearly displaying its LSWR origins. Recorded in its last days as a recognisable station, the debris on the opposite platform and lack of obvious passenger information and barrows etc must indicate it is no longer in the public timetable. The date then is between June 1963, when passenger services were withdrawn, and November 1966 when the signal box was taken out of use. Notice too the trailing connection from the up siding west, similarly it is some time since it was last used.*

Tony Woodforth collection

Rear cover: *Eaking out its last months of revenue earning service 'N' No 31408 is recorded near Hinton Admiral on a warm summers day, 12th August 1965. (See also page 65 of Issue 7).*

Julian Bowden collection

OAKLEY

a simple wayside stopping place - blink and it's gone.

Five miles west of Basingstoke, on the main line to Salisbury, there was, until June 1963, the small stopping place of Oakley. The railway here is of course still open and whilst the area may indeed have developed much over the past years, Oakley together with its three surrounding villages still in 2009, account for a population of only some 5,500 souls. Small wonder then that even now there would be difficulty in justifying a station let alone during those savage sabre wielding days 40+ years ago.

As a stopping place the station had a life of 107 years, being opened in April 1856 just two years after the original single line from Worting Junction had been extended west. It would be reasonable to assume the goods yard was opened around the same time, whilst doubling of the main line took place from the east in December 1861 and then west to Whitchurch in June 1866. It would be fascinating to know the working of the station around this period, as the first mention of a signal box was not until 1872.

For the subsequent 80 years the station was operating, little in the way of change took place, although one amusing incident is recalled in 'Main Line to the West - Part 1': "16th October 1895. The Engineering Committee had reported that on the 7th and 9th September Sir Edward Bates' gamekeeper had been found ferreting for rabbits on the slopes of the cuttings between Worting Junction and Oakley. This was referred to the company solicitor."

The accompanying photographs were submitted by Dave Barker, with thanks also to David Airey and Dave Richards.

Opposite top - *Viewed towards Basingstoke. The photograph shows the then common practice of including a dip in the platform the purpose of which was to facilitate staff passage between the platforms, and which was thus conveniently located opposite the doors to the main building. This provision was altered and the slope raised to uniform level on instructions from the Traffic Officers' Conference of 23rd July 1914, "due to problems alighting from modern types of carriages." From 1914 onwards, a board crossing was provided at the west end of the station and used by both staff and passengers: no footbridge was ever provided. (Between Basingstoke and Salisbury, the stopping places at Oakley, Hurstbourne, and Idmiston Halt all required passengers to cross the running lines in like fashion.) According to Nicholas and Reeve in 'Main Line to the West - Part 1', passengers could leave the down platform from a pathway leading to bridge No 147, seen in the middle distance, although this is not obvious from (located) photographs. Facilities on this platform were limited to a single timber waiting shelter. The view here probably dates from around 1900, as witness the ballast covering of the sleepers. The timber boarding between the rails directly opposite the signal box was intended as some form of protection to the rodding at this point. The station was slightly less than 2½ miles from Worting Junction and just over three miles from Overton. It was from the latter point that supervision was exercised after the abolition of the station master post at Oakley in the mid-1920s. Behind the camera was a trailing connection from the up main line into what was known as 'Up Siding West'. Several coal pens faced on to this siding which also continued for a short distance to form a loading dock behind the up platform terminating at the signal box. The loading dock had been extended to this point shortly after July 1914 and the photograph pre-dates this change - it is perhaps easier seen in the view overleaf. At the opposite, eastern end of the site, were the main goods facilities: a further goods siding and dock on the up side, with trailing connections at either end and, from 1893, a small goods store. Two trailing crossovers, one at each end of the site, and a refuge siding on the down side of the line, accessed again by a trailing connection, completed the facilities. This then was Oakley at its peak, no additions being made at any time until closure.*

Opposite bottom - *Seen from the approach road, which was itself gated and led up from what is nowadays the B3400. The main building was on the up side of the line and as well as affording accommodation for the usual offices, was home to the resident station agent - the reference 'station master' was a later term. To the left the driveway continued towards a weigh bridge, goods office and cattle pen, the latter a small facility standing on top of the dock facing 'Up Siding East'. Prior to February 1899 there had also been a wagon turntable on the site. The station building itself dated from 1862 and was to the design of Joseph Bull, similar to that seen at nearby Overton. The view here is believed to date from LSWR days, at which stage the window on the first floor above the entrance had been sealed. In Southern Railway days, bill boards were attached to the walls either side of the entrance porch and a large 'SR' enamel sign placed on the wall between the ground and first floor windows on the right.*

Slightly later than that depicted on the previous page and with the loading dock at the end of 'Up Siding West' and also the sleepers more pronounced. Notice to the seemingly hotch-potch addition of building between the signal box and station buildings.

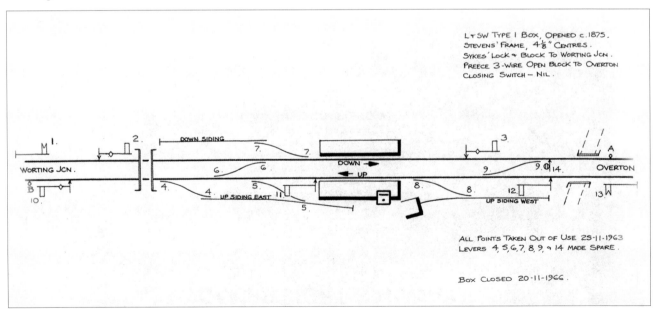

An undated signal diagram from George Pryer but possibly applicable throughout the life of the station and signal box. Unusual, but certainly not unique, is the seemingly total lack of ground discs, in and out of the various sidings: similarly, with one exception, disc No 14, for the trailing crossovers between the main lines. All these movements were in fact under the control of point discs, operating in conjunction with the movement of the turnout. The rationale for this saved lever space and simplified the locking.

OAKLEY

Top right - *Under the canopy on the up side. As opened in April 1856, there was only a single platform on the down side, the main brick building, which still survives in 2009, being added in 1862.*

Centre - *The neat facilities with the main yard and down refuge siding at the east end of the site are seen here to advantage. Traffic inwards was primarily coal, also mixed goods needed for the local area. Outwards would be sent agricultural produce of various types. The station did have one regular VIP passenger between the years 1861 and 1902. This was Wyndham S. Portal who rose to become Chairman of the LSWR. The connection with the LSWR was continued by his son Sir William Portal up to 1922.*

Below - *In this view, the previously referred to point-discs, probably of Stevens' manufacture can be seen - seemingly painted white to the rear. The cattle pens are also visible. A practice at Oakley, possibly common on the LSWR, was for the signalman to ring a hand bell to indicate to station staff the imminent arrival of a train. Passenger traffic came from boys to and from nearby Hilsea College and of course shoppers to the Basingstoke Friday market.*

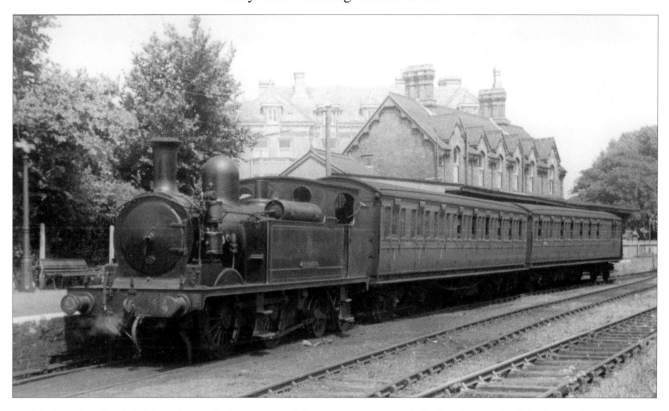

In this 'Rolling Stock File' we have a look at some of the compartment stock designed by each of the 3 constituent companies of the Southern.

Photo 1 - opposite top: In preparation for possible use in its electrification schemes, the South Eastern and Chatham Railway built 66 high capacity coaches in the closing years of its life. These vehicles had 10 compartments in an overall body length of 60ft 1in. and seated 100 people. In the event, they did not feature in the electrification programme and remained steam-hauled throughout their lives. Here we see S 1097 S, delivered in November 1922; one of the batch of 20 with SECR-built bodies and underframes built by the Birmingham RC&W Co. to SECR diagram S2811/4. Originally SECR number 1415, it was renumbered 1097 in 1929 and allocated SR diagram 52. These coaches spent most of their SR days formed into sets often designated for 'Special Traffic', where their large seating capacity was much appreciated. From the early 1950s, many of these vehicles became loose coaches, available to strengthen trains as required. No 1097, which became a loose coach in 1952, is seen here at Sheerness on 8th August 1954 awaiting its next call of duty. It was withdrawn in August 1961 and found its way to the coach dump on the Ardingly branch before being dispatched to Newhaven for breaking up. The last coaches survived on the Lancing Workman's Train until October 1963. Sister coaches 1098 and 971 are preserved on the Bluebell Railway.

Photo 2 - opposite bottom: This is a lovely view of ex-LSWR 3rd lavatory coach S616 at Redhill on 22nd June 1952. This coach was built in September 1909 as 2nd/3rd Composite no 886 (LSWR Drawing 1302) forming part of a 4-coach 'mainline set'. It was renumbered 3013 and, along with the other 2nd/3rd composites, was downgraded to all 3rd around 1916-20, changing its number again to 861. In Southern days it became no 616 (SR Diagram 17) and was in Set No 138. Sometime around 1936, the 4-coach sets had the 3rd removed, becoming now 3-coach sets and retaining their formations until withdrawn in the 1950s. No 616 became a loose coach at this time, strengthening trains as required. It was withdrawn in June 1957.

Photo 3 - above: In this view we see an ex LBSCR 2-coach set at Bembridge IOW on 24th May 1953. This is almost certainly IOW set 505 which was allocated to the branch at that time. It was built in 1911 as one of four push-pull sets for the Brighton-Worthing services. The set was numbered 995 in early SR days, becoming 728 in 1937. It was modified and transferred to the Island as set 505 in 1947. It comprises 7-compartment Brake 3rd no 4167 (SR no 3825) to IOW diagram 231 (SR Diagram 189) and Composite no 6366 (SR no 6201) to SR & IOW diagram 346. The composite has three first and six third-class compartments and both vehicles have a side corridor. Although push-pull fitted it is not in use in this mode, as the locomotive, W14, is not equipped for push-pull operation. After the branch closed on 21st September 1953, the coaches were dumped at St Helens Quay where they remained until broken up in 1956. The two surviving sets on the mainland lasted until 1959/60.

(All photos Terry Cole collection)

BRIGHTON 1903, 1890 and 1933

We are delighted to present a short pictorial appraisal of Brighton commencing on this page with the railway bridge over Trafalgar Street. It had appeared in this form consequent upon the rebuilding of the station that took place in 1882/83. It was from this time that the characteristic awning, or perhaps more accurately described 'porte-cochère' and meaning an awning to admit a vehicle and also give shelter to anyone alighting form it, was provided. Responsibility for the roof design of the rebuilt station and so presumably the awning also, being that of H E Wallis. A notice on the platform invites passengers to alight "..down the steps to Trafalgar Street and the North East Part of the Town", presumably the curved exit-way on the left just visible under the bridge. Evidence of passing horse traffic is present whilst graffiti is clearly not just a recent phenomenon.

Right - The cab rank in nearby Terminus Road, the appropriately named Railway Street is on the left. The west side of the station is on the right, meaning this queue would be of some length crossing Trafalgar Street immediately behind where the photographer was standing for the view on page 12, before continuing the short distance to the front of the station. B K Cooper in his book 'Railcentres Brighton', suggests the cabs visible may have been waiting summons from other locations in the town, hotels and the like. If so it would have required the services of a 'runner' to summon a cab from the front of the queue.

BRIGHTON 1903, 1890 and 1933

Opposite page, main view - Not strictly railway related, but who could resist including this view of the town looking down Queens Road towards the beach. The scene is contemporary with the view on the previous page. Queens Road was built in 1845 to connect the new railway terminus, behind the photographer, with North Street and West Street.

This page - We now move backwards a few years to an interior view of the station in the 1890s. No doubt deliberately taken around mid-day and possibly from the vantage referred to in the caption below, the photographer has managed to persuade, or perhaps even arrange, for most of those present to pose for the requisite time required. Identified on Platform 1 is what is probably a 'D' class 0–4–2T attached to a train of 4 or 6-wheeled stock, all of which, plus the other vehicles in the station, are oil lit. Gas lamps hang from the roof whilst on Platform 3 a man appears to be working on the roof of a road box of some description which is standing on the carriage shoot.

Opposite page, insert - To conclude, we move forward in time to 5th June 1933. This was referred to in the original notes accompanying the photograph as the 'Operations Centre' for Brighton but is more likely the location of the station announcer. Those present would appear to be installing equipment, notice the test meter on the ground. When subsequently operational, messages on train arrivals and departures would be received from the signal box and platform inspectors, to be relayed in suitable 'tinned speech' fashion to waiting passengers.

Photographs - RCHS-Spence Collection - 4, and Corbis - 1.

Above - From the air between 1932 and 1935. The buildings are identified as 'A'; Dining Room with kitchen behind, 'B' - Gymnasium, 'C' - Lodge House, 'D' - Billiard Room and Day Room, 'E' - Hospital Block, this is still extant as part of the care home. Note the covered walkway linking the main building with the Hospital Block, the boys and girls wards were segregated one on either side, 'F' - Main entrance, 'G' - Laundry, 'H' - Boy's playing field, and 'I' the Board Room.
Below - Children from the home on the up platform at Woking , July 1924. Obviously at outing the destination for which was not recorded. The segregation between the sexes will be noted.

The Southern Railway Servants Orphanage

also known as:

'WOKING HOMES'

From notes provided by Mavis E Phair, Ellen Rudkin, Barry Coom and others

To thousands of travellers it was the large building facing the railway on the London side of Woking station, but to hundreds of others it was literally home.

Located a mile from the actual station at Woking, the origins of what started as the 'London & South Western Railway Servants Orphanage' go back almost 125 years, to 1885, when the Rev. Canon Allen Edwards M.A., Vicar of All Saints Church, Lambeth and also Railway Chaplin, rented a large terrace house, No. 76 Jeffreys Road, Clapham, as a home to ten fatherless girls from railway families. Initially this had come about purely through the good offices of Canon Edwards, who as Railway Chaplin of Nine Elms, took a special interest in the large number of railwaymen in his parish, encouraging them to assist each other during times of adversity. One of his railwayman parishioners had his family of small daughters left homeless in consequence of the death of their father and it was this that had provided the catalyst for the rental of No. 76. Both the rental costs and that of a resident housekeeper were at the time being paid for by Canon Edwards, but he must also have been a persuasive man, for he was quick to convince some of the railwaymen then at Nine Elms that they should both take and develop his ideas. The first children became resident in 1886. A Board of Managers was quickly appointed and with funds subscribed mainly from LSWR staff, the Board made the brave decision to not only purchase the freehold of the property but also to expand into the next door house as well, the number of girls by this time needing accommodation having also grown to 50.

Here matters rested, until 1895 at least, when the then LSWR General Manager, Sir Charles Scotter, donated £500 to perpetuate the memory of his wife, who had herself taken a keen interest in the work. This donation allowed the purchase of a third house, this time for 26 boys, the destiny of these unfortunates prior to this time not being recorded.

Seeing the action of the General Manager, the LSWR Directors contributed a further 500 guineas and another large house, this time in Guildford Road, Clapham was acquired in 1900. Guildford Road subsequently became the girls' home, Jeffreys Road being used solely for boys.

Again numbers grew and no doubt with concerns over a piece-meal sanctuary spread over several sites, the decision was made to purchase land for a purpose-built refuge. We do not know where else may have been considered at this time, but something over seven acres were purchased from the London Necropolis Company at Woking (the same organisation that had managed the cemetery at Brookwood and of course had a station at Waterloo), the new home at Woking being completed and fully operational by 1909. The cost of the move was quoted as having been some £30,000, although it is not known if this included the £2,800 cost of the original land purchase at the site. The accommodation at Clapham is not referred to again so may be presumed to have been sold, although history recalls it was still many years before the cost of the new facility was fully covered. The new facility at Woking could accommodate a maximum of 150 children.

Commensurate with the grouping in 1923, a name change occurred, to the 'Southern Railway Servants Orphanage'.

In the *Southern Railway Magazine*, 'The Orphanage', as it was referred to was kept in the forefront of the minds of staff through regular features in the 'Magazine' over the years. This appears to have been particularly so in the pre-war years. For example, in aid of funds, on January 15th 1929, the 31st Bohemian Concert was held at Cannon Street Hotel with the Southern CME, Mr R E L Maunsell presiding. A report presented at the concert stated that up to that time, 935 fatherless children had been cared for and there were then 71 boys and 55 girls in residence. The Home had taken in children in necessitous cases from the all Southern Railway employees since the time of the grouping. 80% of boys leaving had also found employment on the SR and whilst we cannot be certain if this high percentage was maintained, it was certain that former residents were given priority in railway employment for many years. At that time, January 1929, Mr Arthur Smith was Superintendent at the Home assisted by the Matron, Miss Core. The January concert raised some £320.

Shortly afterwards, on March 2nd 1929 there was the dedication of the Bournemouth Cot, £100 having been raised through the Bournemouth District Committee. As was usual, the visitors were entertained to tea – at which

Probably taken on the same occasion as the previous view., despite the initial impression of a sombre group, close examination reveals several children clearly excited with their outing.

their pockets were again strained with a further £3 5s collected. Mention was also made of the efforts of a Mr Farley at Waterloo and 'his famous dog' who had between them collected a further £11.

So far as the committees were concerned, there is mention of a new group being formed in the late summer of 1929 in the London East Division with F W Slatter of Thornton Heath as Secretary. The area covered was from Victoria south to Oxted, London Bridge to Epsom and Charing Cross to Dartford.

The first expansion after the grouping came on 2nd November 1929 when an £8,000 addition in the form a Memorial Hospital was opened. The name chosen as a tribute to those old boys from the home who had fallen in the Great War. Facilities included separate wards for 12 boys and 12 girls, a single observation ward, operating theatre and nursing accommodation. The whole was in keeping with the architectural style of the original 1909 building. The new building was located on the west side. A gymnasium followed in 1932.

Assisting the orphanage appears to have been an almost daily occurrence to some as was reported in the 'Southern Railway Magazine' at the same time. "Episode

1 – A poor woman at Eastbourne Station wants to get her pram home and not the fare for it. Station staff have a 'whip round' and pay the necessary 3/-. Episode 2 – Station staff, Eastbourne surprised to have 3/- refunded by post, they request Station Master to forward the money to the Orphanage".

Later in October 1934, gifts of produce weighing some 18cwt were raised at the Maidstone 'Pound Day'. Interestingly the 'Magazine' also refers to the home being a 'worthy charity', whilst a few years earlier at Cannon Street, Mr Maunsell had been quoted as saying it was not a 'charitable institution'.

Further development was discussed in 1934, when thoughts turned to an expansion of the main building to form what was in effect a quadrangle. The necessity for this was a simple case of overcrowding, brought about by an influx of children since 1923. Indeed at that time, 1934, the home was reported to have been, "… over-crowded, but fortunately it had not been necessary to refuse admission to anyone so far". The new extension was intended to offer accommodation for 100 extra children (this figure was later revised down to 90) together with living rooms and domestic offices. In addition the dining

Boys exercising outside the main entrance, clearly visible also from the main line. This was likely to have been a staged demonstration, from the attire also prior to the 1932 gymnasium being built.

hall would be extended, storage accommodation 'generously supplemented', the heating system of the existing building 'brought up to date and made thoroughly efficient' and staff accommodation improved. The cost, later stated elsewhere to have been £23,000, was met through borrowing and then 'liquidated' by a general appeal to the whole of the SR staff. The new wing faced Oriental Road and was brought into use in 1935.

Further expansion came in 1937, when a further 2½ acres of land was purchased to be used as a playing field for the girls. Additionally a separate large house, 'Brantwood', across the road from the main building was acquired. Later, in 1946, this became a nursery for the youngest residents. Part of the reason for this expansion was to safeguard the potential of the site, urban development encroaching ever closer.

Still run by a Board of Managers, a new departure came in 1947 when two new buildings, 'Wynberg' and 'Missenden' were opened, this time as sheltered accommodation for retired railwaymen or widows. It was a far-sighted approach although at the time it is doubtful if those in control could have perceived that this would indeed be where the future lay. A separate detached house for the Home Superintendent was provided in the grounds although other staff lived in 'the big house'. The idea of sheltered accommodation for old railway employees had been mooted some years earlier in 1939, by Mr H J O'Neil, then the Chairman of the Board of Management. War-time necessity had caused the delay until 1947.

Post-1935, accommodation at Woking was for about 200 children, the boys and girls strictly segregated except at supervised times. The whole was run very much along the lines of a strict yet caring environment, individual responsibility being as important as the welfare provided.

Even so facilities were good in what was in many respects a self-contained community, whilst it is important also to consider what follows in the context of the times rather than the more liberal attitude to child care as exists decades later.

Within the home it would have been impossible to provide the one-on-one love and attention a child might receive from a parent or guardian at home, but even so every effort was made for the children. The home had for example, a fully equipped library containing

Happy Times at the S.R. Orphanage.

CHILDREN'S CHRISTMAS REJOICINGS.

Gifts of toys, confectionery and fruit poured into the Orphanage at Christmastime in larger quantities than ever from all parts of the Southern Railway system.

The week preceding the holiday was spent in decorating the premises in a colour scheme of yellow and blue on a fine background of holly and laurel. The Matron and her staff excelled in their efforts to make the decorations the best of their experience. The children also took part in the decorating, and needless to say thoroughly enjoyed the work. The Orphanage Hospital was decorated by the Staff Nurse, Miss F. Payne, and her helpers, with effective results.

On Christmas Eve the staff, headed by the

officials and friends attended to carve and serve the meal. Amongst those present were the two Hon. Chaplains, the Rev. J. Clifford Banham and the Rev. F. Middleton Price, and their wives, Mr. and Mrs. Pheby, senior and junior, Mr. G. H. Hopgood, Mr. J. Hopgood, the Matron and Staff of the Woking Maternity Home, Dr. K. L. J. Scott, Medical Officer, Mr. W. H. Gower, Miss E. Twigg, Mr. A. E. Smith (Secretary-Superintendent) and Mrs. Smith and Miss M. Core (Matron).

After dinner the children received parcels from their friends, and in those cases where there are no relatives Railwaymen from all parts of the system had arranged to send a parcel so that no child went without a gift.

The Southern Railway Servants' Orphanage, Woking (an aerial view).

Secretary-Superintendent, engaged in the pleasurable task of filling stockings, although it is to be feared that in spite of their quietness and the lateness of the hour many stockings were very soon raided and a midnight "feed" engaged in by some children.

On Christmas morning the children paid their customary visit to the quarters of the Secretary-Superintendent, Matron and Staff, and roused them from bed at a very early hour by singing carols. Christmas greetings were made at breakfast in time-honoured fashion.

The event of the day, Christmas dinner, was served piping hot at the right moment by the kitchen staff, to whom everyone gave unstinted praise for their efforts. As usual, various

During the evening the children entertained each other with items from the concert by themselves. The entertainment was excellent and reflected great credit on the staff who had the onerous task of training the actors.

On Boxing Day the children spent the day in playing with the toys they received on the previous day, and in the evening were again entertained by other items from their repertoire of concert material. This was followed by a party for the elder children, who indulged in games and dancing until bedtime.

Altogether the holiday can be described as the best ever known. To the friends who contributed so generously the Board of Management extend their sincere appreciation.

February, 1934.

Page 73

An example, this one from the February 1934, 'Southern Railway Magazine' of how the Home was kept in the mind of the staff on a regular basis. Indeed, during the inter-war years a feature or comment, not always a full page of course, would appear in most monthly issues.

encyclopaedias, books on nature subjects as well as Shakespeare, Dickens and other classics. All of these were donated by local committees of the Southern Railway and its successor the Southern Region, whose members might also sponsor a bed in one of the dormitories. When television was provided later, one set for 240 children up to the late 1970s, they were restricted to three hours per week, part of which must be of documentary material. As

might be expected some skylarking did occur, the senior boys, (senior boys and girls had their dormitories on the top floor, respectively left and right of the main entrance). One former resident recalling one occasion when one of the boys was smoking and the 'stooge' announced a member of staff was approaching. As was usual practice everyone made a dive for a bed, it did not matter whose, as the appearance would be of a quiet and settled group. On

The Memorial Hospital, opened in 1932.

this occasion the boy with the cigarette quickly placed the stub between his toes before jumping between the sheets – unfortunately he managed to set his bed on fire in the process, fortunately without serious consequences. On another occasion two boys unintentionally jumped into the same bed simultaneously, but it was not noticed. As seniors, the boys and girls were afforded some degree of privacy, with a curtain surrounding their beds, a bedside locker, chair and wooden cabinet with drawers. Part of the Saturday morning regime was to polish the furniture within one's own cubicle.

An in-house laundry complete with the latest equipment for the period was provided, whilst there was also a resident cobbler to take care of the children's footwear. All were issued with the same, two pairs of laced leather shoes, three pairs of plimsolls, one for indoors, one for gym and one for school, Wellington boots and sports shoes.

The day would start with the ringing of the bell at 7.00 am, apparently used by much of Woking as their own early morning wake up call as well. The Woking townsfolk were also known to write letters of complaint to the Principal should the bell be out of commission at any time.

Although privately run, former staff refer to the regime as similar to an 'upper class boarding school', with regular Home Office inspections as indeed then applied to any similar management-run institution. In this respect Woking was always highly regarded. (Other welfare schemes for disadvantaged railwaymen's children were in place on the LNER and LMS, the latter in the form of a smaller, although similarly designed home, St Christopher's, at Derby. During the 1950s and 1960s sports days and competitions took place between the homes, whilst the athletic and gymnastic prowess of some of the Woking children was such that they were judged to be at county level.

But to run a home of this type was expensive and railway staff were encouraged to donate 2d-3d (old money), from their wages weekly. Even so this would only cover perhaps 75% of the actual running costs. Further funds were raised by running excursions by any one of 16 welfare committees scattered around the Southern. Additionally money was raised by a number of dogs, whose job was to walk the major stations and sometimes the trains, complete with collecting box strapped to their backs. These dogs and their handlers, were on the railway payroll, each dog receiving a medal to commemorate each complete year of collecting service. At the end of their lives, the animal suffered the indignity of a visit to a taxidermist to be then placed in a glass case on a station and further continue its collecting role.

Whilst at nursery level, boys and girls were in mixed groups, although after the age of six segregation took place into groups of between 17- 20 children first as Juniors, then Lower Senior and finally Senior, so far as boys were concerned there was also an intermediate group, known as 'inters' after junior.

Any parent who has been faced with providing for children so far as clothing is concerned will appreciate the children at Woking were in fact well equipped. Attire consisted of a 'best' for Sunday church wear, Saturday clothes and play clothes. Each was either discarded when worn out, or cascaded down to a smaller child as they were outgrown. In addition there were three sets of school clothing, PE kit and a separate Gym kit for use in the Woking gymnasium.

Following the wake-up bell, which rang at the same time every day including weekends, the routine was, beds stripped and blankets folded, strip wash and then breakfast at 7.30 am. Next. prayers were said at 7.55 am, the younger children learning by listening to the older children as well as by repetition. At random a section was asked to repeat one of the ten commandments - all used to

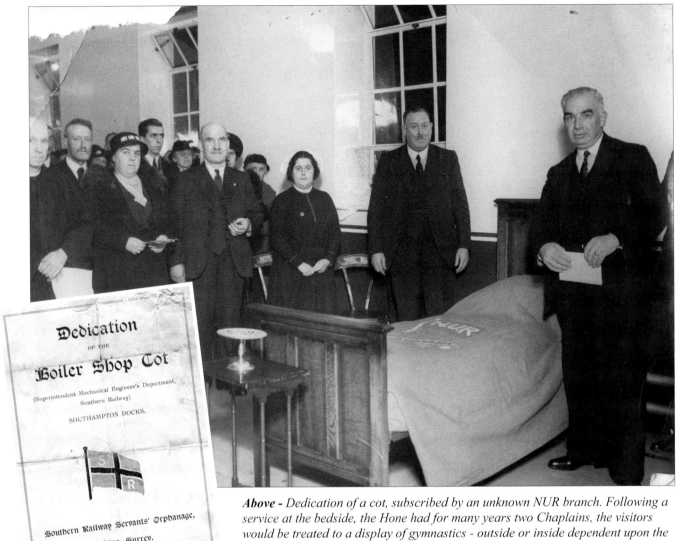

Above - Dedication of a cot, subscribed by an unknown NUR branch. Following a service at the bedside, the Hone had for many years two Chaplains, the visitors would be treated to a display of gymnastics - outside or inside dependent upon the weather and then tea in the dining room. Invariably a collection would be held, with those present encouraged to 'give generously'.

Inset - Although unrelated to the above view, it was the practice produce a small brochure - a form of service sheet, for these occasions. Included would be the programme of events and hymns to be sung.

Right - Some of the endowed cots from the committees and others. The committees endowed the beds with ornamental quilts and plaques as new beds were required. Each committee would send a representative to Woking to form what was the Board of Management.

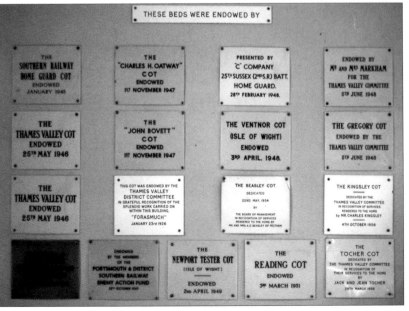

Gymnastics display for summer visitors. In the background the tall chimney was for the Parazone factory. Another commercial factory nearby was that of the GQ Parachute Works.

Children attending secondary schools were required to listen to the news on the BBC Home Service each weekday evening. To ensure attention was paid, questions were asked by the Secretary Superintendent the next day.

Summer camp at Elmer Sands near Bognor. At one time in the 1960s, the home had use of a modified Bedford mini-bus type vehicle, the body work for which was box-shaped and may well have been provided in one of the railway workshops. At camp the different tents were occupied by different groups, boys and girls in the ridge tents, staff in bell tents and the marquee for dining. The children were also expected to participate in household chores at camp. Ellen (Laird) is seated by the table in the foreground.

hope to get No. 8, the shortest, and not the 3rd, the longest! Each child was then allocated a chore, it might be washing up or sweeping prior to lining up ready for the walk to school. Schooling was not provided on site and instead local schools were used. One of the schools used, involved a walk of over a mile along Oriental Road, left into Maybury Hill and then left again into Maybury Road before reaching Maybury School almost opposite the home itself. It has been suggested that during the early days a footbridge may have been provided from the home immediately across the railway to form an easier and quicker access, but when this was removed is not recorded. Dependent upon the education attainment of the children following the 11+ exam, some would return to the home for lunch, immediately followed by more washing-up. Tea was served at 4.30 pm with homework at 6.00 pm. Shoes also had to be cleaned daily whilst every Friday a

sack of shoes was delivered from the cobbler's shop, the children expected to swap between their pairs of shoes weekly and thus even out wear.

Outside interests and pursuits were encouraged, especially those involving organisations such as Scouting and Guides, whilst gym attendance was compulsory at least once a week. Swimming lessons took place in the summer with an outside instructor, all the children being taught to swim. This same man taught ballroom and modern dancing to the seniors on Friday evenings, the only time the sexes were encouraged to have anything like close physical contact. Sunday morning all the children attended church whilst in the afternoon the children were expected to write a letter home; not surprisingly a number may have found this a rather challenging task. Also on Sunday afternoon and except during poor weather, it was compulsory to go for a walk for around two hours before

Left - Ritual duties at camp.

Below - The billiard and day had, at one end, an 'O' gauge model railway, it is believed there may also have been a ground level live-steam line around the grounds at some time at well. In what is clearly a posed view, the boy is delighted with his new acquisition. The adults are not recognised and so may well have been visiting relatives. The Home originally took children from age 6 caring from them until age 14 later 16. Upon leaving they were issued with a new set of clothes and would be provided with further welfare support, if necessary until aged 21. Aside from long term accommodation, children were also temporarily admitted such as due to illness of one or both parents. The parents of children taken due to separation or divorce were expected to contribute to the cost of maintenance.

Mr Parker in the cobbler's shop from where a bag of shoes issued each week so that the children might rotate their footwear to even out wear. The cobbler would also teach his craft to any of the youngsters if they showed an interest.

tea. Now the children were free to go where they wished although still subject to certain areas considered to be 'out of bounds'.

Otherwise discipline was strict, corporal punishment being meted out if necessary. One relaxation was on birthdays, also the only day when post was permitted at the breakfast table – otherwise it was given out just prior to leaving for school. Birthdays were special in that the child was permitted a private birthday tea, able to invite two friends from school in addition to any siblings also resident. Apart from this time, it was only if a family member visited, (family visits were monthly), or at Christmas, when brothers and sisters might eat together.

Reference has already been made to the work of the various local committees in fund raising and sponsorship, whilst another practical achievement was in the form of organised outings. These took place throughout the year and were organised again in age order, the senior boys making a regular visit to Southampton for lunch on one of the Cunard 'Queens' as well as having a trip on a smaller boat around Southampton water. Younger children went to the Huntley and Palmer biscuit factory at Reading, whilst an optional outing was to an ice show. Additionally, at Whitsun there was a camping holiday at Elmer Sands, near Bognor, all travelling by train - of course, - from Woking to Barnham changing at Havant,

with the final part of the journey by Southdown bus. Other outings were to Bournemouth for tea with the Mayor and a trip around the bay, Osborne House and other places of interest. Theatre came from the Railway Dramatic Society who would perform their dress rehearsals at Woking with a similar presentation by various Welsh Male Voice Choirs.

The prelude to Christmas saw invitations issued to the children to attend Railwaymen's parties all over the Southern region. There was also a regular Christmas trip to Bertram Mills Circus, courtesy of the *Daily Sketch*. On Christmas Eve there was a much looked forward to visit by the Salvation Army to each dormitory. Here a Pillow Fight was allowed between the visitors and residents. Later on Christmas Eve there was a carol service from the Salvation Army whilst those who could not go home for Christmas, were given a stocking for their bed – waking up to find it filled on Christmas morning, again courtesy of the committees. Good deeds were not forgotten even at Christmas, as the older children performed carols at the old people's homes before breakfast. This was followed by church and then lunch, ending with the Christmas pudding served by the male staff in fancy dress. As recounted, Christmas Day was when brothers and sisters resident might be permitted to sit together.

Christmas Day afternoon saw family presents

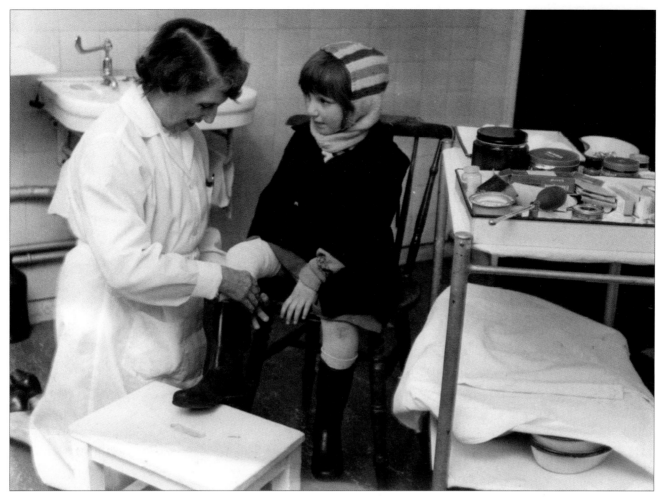

Opposite top - The sewing room, both sexes were expected to assist if required. This was located on the first floor, right hand side - when viewed from the front of the building. *Opposite bottom* - The dining hall. Pictures of the various patrons hung from the wall. *Above* - Part of the hospital block. *This page, bottom right* - Plaque from the main building no doubt intended to encourage the children to succeed. The actual decorations appear not to have been photographed.

distributed after which each child was expected to write thank-you letters. The festivities continued with a party, Father Christmas was in attendance of course, and each child was presented with a gift, again supplied by the committees.

Outside organisations were also welcome benefactors. Thornton's the chocolate manufacturer donated several of their demonstration two-inch-thick chocolate Easter Eggs to be broken up and shared by the children.

With changing times, the word 'Orphanage' was removed from the title in the mid 1960s and instead it became 'Woking Grange' – it very nearly became 'Primrose Hill', although outside it was often still referred to by the original names by railway staff.

There was certainly no intention to cease the original functions of the home right through to the 1980s, although a change to the ratio of staff to children now required by social services made continuing in its original guise too expensive to continue. The final seven children resident moved into a new smaller children's home, 'The Foxes' in August 1988, although all of these had departed

by the summer of the following year.

Instead the site has taken on a new lease of life and whilst the original building of 1909 has been demolished and part of the land sold off, an expansion of the elderly residents' home means there is now accommodation for 50 retired railway staff, many with private en-suite accommodation. A link with the past has also been retained in naming a number of the buildings that remain after former stalwarts of the home. The original children's hospital, by the 1970s known as 'Grace Groom House', was also converted to a new use as part of this accommodation.

These British and Foreign decorations and medals and personal gifts from our own Royal Family, were gained by

MR EDWIN CHARLES COX

who rose, during an illustrious career of over 50 years, from messenger boy to Traffic Manager of the Southern Railway Before he died on 10th December 1958, Mr Cox asked that his decorations should be displayed here at the Southern Railways Servants Orphanage to demonstrate that however humbly a career may begin, much can be achieved in the end.

Above - *During World War 2, the Home was evacuated and given over to St Thomas's Hospital, the children from the home being billeted with railway families in the surrounding area. As mentioned in the text, the children were encouraged to participate in outside activities which included the Sea Cadet Unit. Here, Richard Brown, just visible wearing the cap, is instructing the boys in the working of a naval gun, thought to be sited in the grounds of the unit clubhouse in Woking Park.*

Left - *The decorative headstone above the main entrance commemorating the founder. Within the library was a brass collection box known as the 'Love Fund' Children were educated to make donations into this box and once a year, believed to have been on Maundy Thursday, each child was presented with 3d. They were then designated to share this, 1d to the church, 1d for the Love Fund and 1d for themselves. The money collected from the Love Fund went towards purchasing gifts for the needy.*

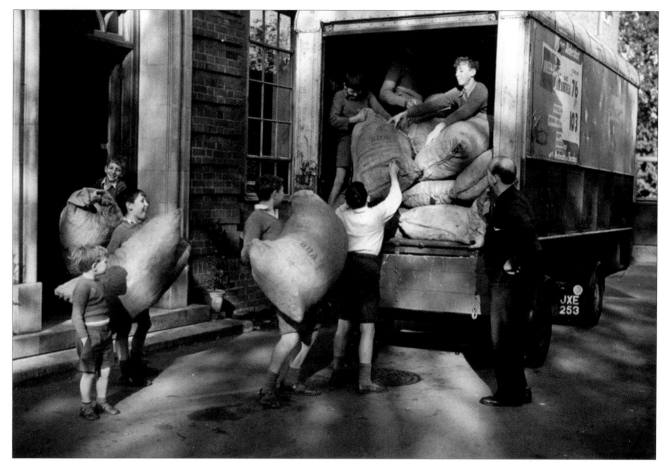

Above - *Recycling 1950s / 1960s style. The home acted as collecting point for the local area for silver foil and other contemporary recyclable items. These were stored in the basement and removed at regular intervals. Those that assisted, seen here is an 'intermediate' boys group, recall the smell associated with the milk bottle tops being loaded. In another area of the basement was a kitchen store where large tins and jars were kept.*

Right - *Ablutions! At this age these young ones, known as 'pickles' had just moved over into the main house from Brantwood Nursery. (1965)* **Below** - *The decorative mosaic tiling inside the main entrance. The colours were white, black, blue and brown fading through to shades of orange and gold. Like the headstone opposite, it did not survive demolition.*

Above - *Modern times.*

Left - *David and Susan Lehuray (seated) with Mr Evershed, Secretary Superintendent, stood behind Susan. The gentleman standing on the left has not been positively identified but may have been from Weymouth. The date was 1975 and was taken to record the presentation of a bench upon the death of the children's father, a railwayman from Weymouth.*

A number of films and local publications feature the home. Details are available at

http://www.woking-grange.co.uk/

and where links are also available to a photo gallery of former residents.

Above - The general office and switchboard in 1959. Mr Wells, the then Secretary Superintendent and who occupied the East Lodge House, is seen on the right.

Right - Grace Groom., former Matron.

Below - Foundation corner stone.

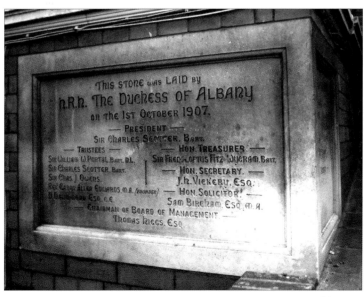

Top left - Class 73 No. 73134 which carried the name 'Woking Homes' from October 1985 until withdrawal in April 1990.

Above right - Barry Coom, resident at Woking Homes and whose idea it was for an article on the history. A reunion of former residents is also planned for October 2009. Further details from tcharliefrancister@yahoo.co.uk

Left - It was not always the children who were involved in the housework!

Woking Homes is now a Registered Charity, No 1120447 and of course welcomes donations.

An annual reunion takes place at Eastleigh Railway Club on the third Saturday of October each year.

This section of 'SW8', dealing with Woking Homes, has also been printed as a separate booklet for the benefit of the Charity. It is being sold by them to raise funds.

Right - *A final glance during a relaxing time. In an attempt to prepare the children for all aspects of life in the outside world, ballroom dancing was compulsory. Some of the boys recall loathing this, not assisted perhaps by being clamped to the rather ample bosom of the then matron.*

Underneath each bed was a basket in which the children would leave their day-clothes. Thus at night and in the event of a fire, it would be possible to evacuate the home rapidly and safely with a set of day cloths each. This same basket was used for nightclothes and dressing gown during the day. A wardrobe room was located on each floor with access to the floors by any one of six staircases.

Insert - *Block from the 'Southern Railway Magazine'. At other times a frontal drawing of the main building was used.*

ORPHANAGE

"A Few Memories Of my Time Spent at S.R.S.O. - Ellen Rudkin (nee Laird).

"It was a warn summers day, 1956 as I remember, I struggled off the bus at Woking with my suitcase. I stood at the top of Oriental road and wondered if I would make it down to the Orphanage. When I eventually reached my destination I was welcomed by Miss Groom and given a cup of tea! Later on I was taken across the road to Brantwood nursery and shown to my bedroom.

"The happy days I spent at the Orphanage were about to begin. I loved working in the nursery with the babies and toddlers; it was hard work and we were kept on our toes by the lady in charge. She would check the bathrooms and bedrooms at night to make sure we had tidied away and cleaned the bathrooms. If the work had not been completed to her satisfaction, she would knock on our bedroom door and we would be told to do it again! Whenever the weather allowed, we had tea in the garden. The children really enjoyed this and would play until it was time to go in for baths.

"One day I received a message from Miss Groom to say she would like to see me in her office. Miss Groom offered me a job working with the older children, as a relief in the first instance and later possibly to take over the responsibility of running the Intermediate Boy's group. Although I felt sad at leaving Brantwood, I was looking forward to working with the older children. Miss Groom had explained to me that because of my age, I was 19 at the time, the salary scales would need to be changed to allow a younger member of staff to be paid!

"On the first day of the transfer , I was shown into the staff room and introduced to another young member of staff, Barbara Mills. We were to remain firm friends and have remained so all these years.

"As it happened, it was not long before I took over the running of the Intermediate Boys: 21 of them as I recall. My time spent looking after the boys turned out to be both happy and rewarding and lots of fun".

Above - *Looking east from St Johns Local platforms in 1913, two Lewisham trains are passing on the left. The truncated No. 1 road can be seen on the right. The steel-plated bridge carries the LC&DR branch to Greenwich Park. The wooden signal bracket carries the Down Through starter. The original SER signal box is in the vee of the junction and there are over 200 telegraph insulators on four tall poles. The platform lamp is oil and the purpose of the concrete post is uncertain.*
H.J.Patterson, Rutherford Collection, reproduced from Reference 7

Above - *From the same location in August 1958, a Ramsgate to Charing Cross train is headed by rebuilt class WC Pacific No. 34021* Dartmoor. *The overhead telegraph and the LC&DR bridge are long gone and just one truss remains of the 1929 flyover. The four-aspect colour-light signal on the right was the one passed at red by the Ramsgate train in the 1957 accident; unlike its SE&CR predecessor, it is not bracketed over the track.*

John Scrace

ST JOHNS STATION, LEWISHAM

HISTORY, MYSTERY & CONNECTIONS

ALAN POSTLETHWAITE

The Metamorphosis of Lewisham

Until the Industrial Revolution, Lewisham was an idyllic village in the wide valley of the gentle rivers Ravensbourne and Quaggy. The village was a mile long, scattered along the broad road towards Sevenoaks (today's A21). Wealthy businessmen lived in substantial houses and could commute to the City by coach. Working-class occupations were a mix of farming, servicing the wealthy and light industries which included milling, tanning, a brewery, a pottery and an armoury. On an outcrop of chalk to the north, the Dover Road ran across Blackheath beyond which was the Royal hunting ground of Greenwich Park. The one major industry was shipbuilding at Deptford and Greenwich where many of Nelson's men-of-war had been built. Reference 1 provides a more detailed description of old Lewisham.

When the railways arrived, Lewisham was rapidly transformed from a quiet village into a busy London suburb, almost obliterating its past. Yellow house bricks were fired at the great clay pits of Loampit Vale. Fields became sprawling rows of near-identical houses, mostly semi-detached with indoor sanitation and gas lighting, suitable for smart office workers who commuted to London. St John's church on Loampit Hill belongs to that frantic period of Victorian development, lending its name to a humble railway station nearby.

Dedicated to St John the Baptist and the Holy Trinity, the church was consecrated in 1855. A service of remembrance was celebrated there in December 2007 for those who had died or suffered fifty years previously in the St Johns railway accident. A report of the service in *The Times* was accompanied by a photograph of the collapsed railway bridge (Ref. 2). In the picture, two disused platforms were apparent <u>south</u> of the flyover, a hundred yards or so from the present station. The mystery of these platforms intrigued the author and was the catalyst of this article.

Early Railways

The London & Greenwich was London's first passenger railway. Opening in 1836, it was built on a brick viaduct from London Bridge across the Bermondsey marshes to the west side of Greenwich. Next to arrive in 1839 was the London & Croydon Railway which branched

From the same location post-privatisation, graffiti is abundant, so too are the sycamores which brush the sides of the trains. When the line was resignalled in 1975, the bracket here was restored over the Down Through line. Difficulty of sighting was a contributory cause of the 1957 accident.

off the Greenwich line at Corbetts Lane and followed the course of the old Croydon Canal. The London & Brighton Railway arrived in 1841, using the Croydon's metals as far as Croydon. This was followed in 1842 by the South Eastern Railway which ran on all three of the above companies' metals before turning east at Redhill on to its own line to Dover. In 1845, the SER took a 999 year lease of the London & Greenwich but they remained separate companies until the Southern Grouping of 1923. The Brighton and Croydon companies amalgamated in 1846 to become the LB&SCR.

This rapid development signalled the start of the Railway Mania. The approach tracks to London Bridge soon became congested and the Greenwich company charged the other companies a toll which they regarded as exorbitant. So the Croydon and the SER built a branch line from Corbetts Lane to a new terminus at Bricklayers Arms (named after a pub), opening in 1844. The next development was the SER's North Kent line. Objections were raised to an extension from Greenwich station which might have caused vibration in the Royal Observatory in Greenwich Park so a new line was built which branched from the Greenwich line at North Kent East junction and

ran through Lewisham, Blackheath, Woolwich, Dartford and Gravesend to a temporary terminus at Strood. The North Kent line was fully opened in 1849, followed in 1850 by the SER station at New Cross. Fig. 1 shows railway developments until 1857. Reference 3 offers a more detailed history of the lines and companies.

As the railways grew, the telegraph was introduced for communication between signal boxes. Using bells and indicators with an earth return, single wires were suspended on lineside telegraph poles. This led to the renting of telegraph lines for non-railway uses, including military. By 1913, St Johns had over 200

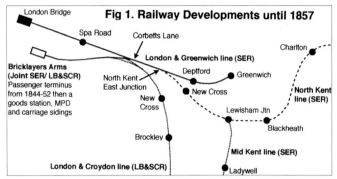

The staff of St Johns in SE&CR days, totalling 14 men and boys, taken on the central island platform looking towards London. Goods wagons are held in the Up Local road (right), including a flat wagon with a covered road cart bearing the name 'George Pyrke'. The valances are plain on the left and SER semi-circular on the right. No canopy or rooms are visible on the north island (far right), this suggests that the old Down platform was being completely rebuilt, dating the picture to around 1903-05 when the line was being quadrupled. New SE&CR valances would have been added to all canopies when the heavy work was near completion.　　　　　　　　　　　　　　　*John Scrace collection*

overhead lines. An early additional role of the telegraph was the transmission of Greenwich Mean Time throughout the world. From 1852, hourly signals were transmitted from the Royal Observatory, originally via the SER at Lewisham. The North Kent line therefore played a key role in the History of Time. It also allowed standard railway time to be introduced for the whole of Britain so that long-distance timetables could become meaningful.

If the Observatory had not objected to an extension of the Greenwich line to the North Kent, then the railways through Lewisham might have developed quite differently. The LB&SCR might have become the dominant company in Lewisham, for example, leaving the SER better placed financially to absorb the embryonic LC&DR in East Kent. We can only speculate how the Kentish railway map might then have evolved.

Developments around St Johns

In 1857, the Mid Kent line opened to Beckenham, worked by the SER. It branched off the North Kent at Lewisham, just short of the old station, so a new Junction station was built, having four platforms in a vee-shape. In order to compete effectively with the up-and-coming London Chatham & Dover Railway, the SER built its main line 'cut-off' via Sevenoaks to Tonbridge. This branched off the North Kent just east of what is now St Johns station, opening to Orpington in 1865 and to Tonbridge in 1868. The Ladywell loop to the Mid Kent was added in 1866 at Parks Bridge junction.

The SER's near monopoly of commuting services around Lewisham was challenged in 1871 with the opening of the LC&DR branch from Nunhead to

Below - The 1 in 45 incline under construction in October 1975. The one remaining platform is the north island; its edge wall is pre-cast concrete, probably rebuilt in 1956 when the platform was extended for 10-car EMUs. Note the heightened road bridge and footbridge to accommodate trains towards the lower end of the incline, also the wooden booking office to their left.

John Scrace

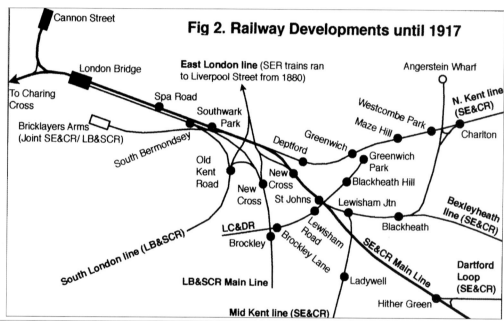

Fig 2. Railway Developments until 1917

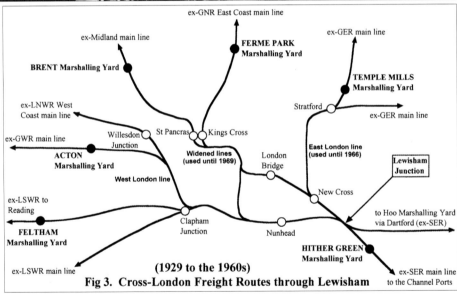

Above - *Resplendent in SR livery, 4-4-0 Schools class V No. 938* St Olaves *heads a 3-coach set of 'birdcage' stock on the Up Through line. A screen hides the remains of the south island platform and the four empty sidings beyond. Note the SE&CR deep valancing.*

H.N.James, reproduced from reference 7.

(1929 to the 1960s)
Fig 3. Cross-London Freight Routes through Lewisham

Blackheath Hill (extended to Greenwich Park in 1888) with intermediate stations at Brockley Lane and Lewisham Road. Not to be outmanoeuvred, the SER responded in 1873 with a new station called St Johns. The SER journey time to the City was about half that of the LC&DR which is why only St Johns remains open. The SER and LC&DR merged operationally in 1899 to become the South Eastern & Chatham Railway. The Greenwich Park branch closed in 1917 as a wartime economy measure, its stations never to reopen. Fig. 2 shows developments in the area to 1917.

During 1903-05, the SE&CR quadrupled its main line from Corbetts Lane to Orpington. Between New Cross and St Johns, this was achieved by excavating the earthen cutting to either side and building retaining walls so that virtually no extra land was required. This explains why Tanners Hill tunnel (to the west of St Johns) has two single-track tunnels to either side of the original double-track tunnel.

In 1923, the SE&CR, LB&SCR, L&SWR and others were grouped into the Southern Railway. Among the rationalisations and improvements that followed, a viaduct and flyover were built in 1929 between Lewisham Junction and the old Lewisham Road station. Also, the Hither Green loop was opened from Lewisham Junction to

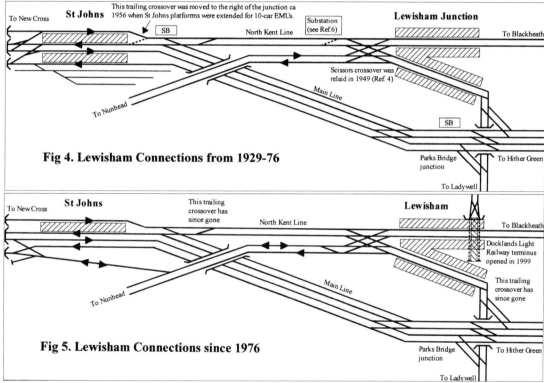

Fig 4. Lewisham Connections from 1929-76

Fig 5. Lewisham Connections since 1976

Above - *At the scene of the 1957 accident, EMU unit 7855 heads the 13.10 Charing Cross to Margate service on 23.10.75. On the Nunhead viaduct and flyover is the 12.15 Northfleet to Toton cement train, headed by a class 33 diesel locomotive. New colour-light signals are awaiting commissioning.*

John Scrace

the main line (Fig. 4). Their purpose was to relieve London Bridge of its goods traffic which had run via Metropolitan Junction to Blackfriars Bridge, the Widened Lines, Kings Cross and St Pancras. A second benefit was to facilitate cross-London freight traffic between Hither Green marshalling yard and the former LSWR, GWR and LNWR via Battersea and the West London line. Fig. 3 shows cross-London freight routes through Lewisham between 1929 and the 1960s. General freight traffic has since declined but bulk mineral trains pass over the Nunhead flyover these days, dedicated to specific industries including aggregates, cement, scrap metal and oil. There are also container trains.

The lines through St Johns were electrified in 1929 for suburban traffic, followed by the Nunhead line in 1933. From 1935, rush-hour services were introduced between the Dartford lines and Blackfriars or Horborn

Viaduct (via Nunhead). This brought further relief to the overcrowding through London Bridge. These days, trains also run to Victoria throughout the day.

St Johns remained a humble commuting station, never in the news until 4th December 1957 when the 4.56 pm Cannon Street to Ramsgate steam train passed several colour-lights at danger in thick fog. It ran through St Johns into the rear of the 5.18 pm Charing Cross to Hayes EMU which was stationary just beyond the Nunhead flyover. The locomotive tender skewed to its left, removing one of the support piers and causing two of the four trusses to collapse onto the train below. Fortunately, the 5.22 pm Holborn Viaduct to Dartford stopped in the nick of time, its leading coach leaning into the carnage but not falling. Ninety people died and it remains the worst accident on the Southern. The flyover was rebuilt and all lines were back in service within six weeks. The 'temporary' rebuilt bridge comprised multiple I-beams with only one of the four original trusses retained. They remain in service to this day. Reference 6 provides a detailed account of the accident and its aftermath.

The convergence of so many SER lines into London Bridge has always led to congestion. Since the 1830s, many measures have been taken to try to ease the constraints of conflicting train movements on these lines. The end of main line steam in 1961 was a great help by eliminating light engine movements. A more recent example (in 1976) is the building of an incline (at a gradient of 1 in 45) from the Nunhead flyover towards New Cross. This carries a single (bi-directional) track to give suburban services additional route options between Lewisham and New Cross, especially in the Up direction (Fig. 5). To accommodate this incline, one span of St Johns Vale road bridge was rebuilt as a flat concrete beam instead of a brick arch. The remaining spans were rebuilt in 1992 (see Ref. 8).

The latest rail link in the area is the Docklands Light Railway which opened to Lewisham in 1999 from Greenwich via Deptford. It terminates at Lewisham, half-covered by the North Kent line and integrated with a bus interchange station.

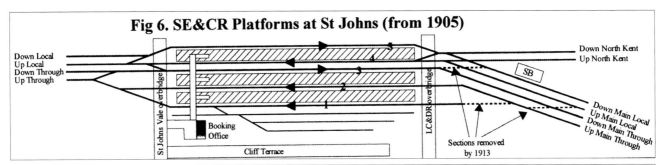

Fig 6. SE&CR Platforms at St Johns (from 1905)

Below Right - *The original signal box was of standard SER wooden construction, sited in the vee of the junction. Its replacement seen here was on the north side of the junction. It entered service in 1929 to control all the lines through Lewisham and St Johns. All signals were colour-lights but points were a mix of mechanical and power operation. A disused LC&DR road bridge is visible above the box, 42 years after closure of the Greenwich Park branch. The box is of early SR brick-to-roof construction with a relay room to the left. On the right are the steps, a closet and the signal linesmen's hut. There is a narrow platform for window-cleaning. Ten window panes have been covered to reduce sun glare and the locking room windows have been bricked up. Three staff are visible in this 1959 picture; at peak times there would be Up and Down signalmen plus booking lads. The box survived until 1976.*

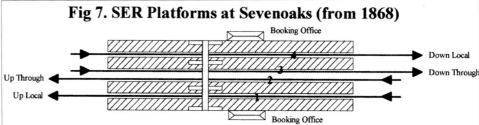

Fig 7. SER Platforms at Sevenoaks (from 1868)

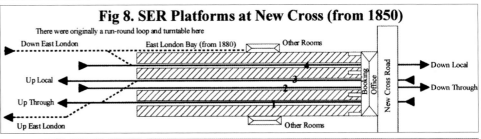

Fig 8. SER Platforms at New Cross (from 1850)

Platforms and Trackwork

For the purposes of this article, the platform roads at St Johns are numbered 1 to 5 from south to north according to the SE&CR platform arrangement of 1905. Actual platform numbering would have changed several times as the number of faces varied from 2 to 6 to 4 and back to 2.

The original St Johns station of 1873 had a conventional two-platform arrangement to either side of the double-track. When the main line was quadrupled in 1903-1905, the two platforms were rebuilt as islands to serve the Local and Through roads respectively. A footbridge at the London end led to a modest booking office at high level off St Johns Vale, close to the church. Curiously, the SE&CR added a third island on the south side and the Up Through was split into parallel roads with No. 2 road having two platform faces (Fig. 6).

One can only speculate as to the intended purpose of the south island at St Johns. The SE&CR may have had in mind the termination of certain off-peak trains in No. 2 road with cross-platform interchange with both Up and Down connecting services. For Mid Kent trains to terminate, however, they would have required either a trailing crossover at the country end or wrong-road working on the Up Through as far as Parks Bridge junction. Such provisions were never installed and No. 1 road remained superfluous throughout its short existence, becoming a bay siding by 1913.

What other comparable stations had extra platform faces? Sevenoaks originally had two extra outside platforms so that Nos. 1 and 4 roads each had two faces (Fig. 7). This gave Local passengers and parcels cross-platform transfer with connecting services on the central Through roads and with the two booking offices and exits at the sides. Such benefits, however, did not apply to the south island at St Johns where the only platform access was by footbridge.

The original New Cross had a similar platform arrangement to Sevenoaks but with a single high-level booking office on the New Cross Road bridge (Fig. 8). The two outer platforms appear superfluous unless they were intended for level access of passengers and parcels using side approaches. When the East London Railway reached New Cross thirty years later, the north outer platform at last acquired a more substantive *raison d'être* by serving the East London bay. So the south platforms at both New Cross and St Johns may be regarded as 'belt and braces' provisions - relics of the Steam Age - there in case they were needed.

Returning to St Johns, Figs. 4 and 6 show provisions for reversing trains in roads 4 and 5 using the trailing crossovers at either end. Their main use was for occasional engineering trains, also for parcels and freight stock to be stored in St Johns' sidings when Bricklayers Arms was full. There is no evidence that they were used for reversing coal trains for Sydenham Gas Works (open

from 1878 to 1969 on the Mid Kent line). Although St Johns offered the shortest route between Erith North Quay and Lower Sydenham, the Southern preferred the longer route via Gravesend, Maidstone West, Tonbridge and Beckenham Junction, often delivering at night. Sydenham coal wagons (from both Erith Quay and all-the-way by rail) were added to general goods trains and were marshalled at Tonbridge, Beckenham Junction and / or Bricklayers Arms. Thanks are due to correspondents from the Southern Railways Group for this information.

Although St Johns No. 1 road soon became a bay siding, its platform remained in service until 1926 when the south island was taken out of use and a screen was erected to prevent passengers alighting. In 1973, the disused island platform was removed together with the middle island so that only the north island remained (serving the Local roads). The four sidings were also removed at that stage as a prelude to straightening the Through lines and construction of the 1 in 45 incline.

The sidings at St Johns were used only for occasional storage and engineering trains. It was never a coal or general goods yard. Indeed, no railway goods yard was ever built in the north Lewisham area - the nearest were at New Cross Gate, Brockley Lane, Blackheath and Catford Bridge. It was a long haul for cart horses to deliver domestic coal hereabouts. It is interesting that domestic coal was generally transported to the South East by rail, particularly from the Midlands, whereas coal for power stations and gas works came mostly by ship from NE England. All contributed generously to the London 'smogs' until abated by the Clean Air Act and modernisation.

Platforms were lengthened a number of times at

The 1992 road bridge spans all four main tracks and the extended island platform. The footbridge beyond rises steeply to clear the 1 in 45 incline. Graffiti artists risk their lives here at night - like climbing the Eiger.

St Johns. The Through island was longer than the Local island until the latter was extended eastwards in 1956 for 10-car EMUs. When St Johns Vale road bridge was rebuilt in 1992 (with a single span), this allowed the platform to be extended westwards for 12-car EMUs, albeit very narrow at the end. Train lengths are currently 4, 5, 8, 10 and 12 car. The high-level booking office has been replaced with a new one on the island platform facing the new footbridge. Some SE&CR valancing remains, also the SE&CR waiting room, now boarded up and used as a storeroom.

Autobiographical Links

Born in July 1940, my first home was in a road called Ladywell Park, just south of the SER main line near Parks Bridge junction. On 17th September 1940, the Luftwaffe dropped the first-ever parachute bombs on London (commonly called 'land mines') from a Heinkel 111. One of them destroyed all twenty-odd houses in Ladywell Park, killing 29 residents. The houses were never rebuilt; these days, it is the site of the new Lewisham Library and Local Studies Centre.

My mother, grandmother and I were buried alive under the stairs. My mother dug us out and we were never accounted for in the records. We were later evacuated to Cheltenham. With the bombing apparently over, we returned in 1944 to live in a house next to Brockley Lane sidings. We immediately lost all our windows due to a V1 flying bomb explosion by the LB&SCR main line. A daily highlight was a tram ride to the Clapham Deep Shelter.

We moved to Catford in 1945 where we stayed until 1958. Public transport and bicycles were our only means of travel. We rode the trams and we climbed the open staircase of quaint ST buses. We could change at New Cross on to an archaic double-deck LT with three axles or on to a modernistic single-deck Q which ran under the low railway bridges of Bermondsey.

In 1957, I started an engineering apprenticeship with the Central Electricity Authority based at Bankside Power Station, now the Tate Modern. So I commuted on the Mid Kent line and attended day-release courses at SE London Technical College at St Johns. I also attended evening classes in Railway History at Goldsmiths College, New Cross, laying the foundations of my secondary career as a railway photographer and author. One of my regular trains home from London Bridge was the Hayes EMU that was involved in the St Johns accident. All trains were running late that evening due to fog which is why I (and a thousand others) were lucky and caught an earlier service.

Looking west from St Johns Vale road bridge, showing Tanner Hill tunnels and the junction of the incline with the Through lines (left). A contemporary 5-car EMU is approaching the Down platform. The author once attended evening classes at the tall LCC school with its great windows.

After graduating in Mechanical Engineering at City University, my first appointment was as a shift engineer at Deptford Power Station. Still in working order was the ancient 25 cycle plant which had originally supplied trams as well as the railway at Lewisham substation when the lines through St Johns were electrified in 1929. This plant was now used only at winter peak periods via a rotary frequency converter called 'The Freak'. My work was in the West turbine house which was built in a dry dock commissioned by Henry VIII for the original Royal Navy. It was haunted by the ghosts of those who had died on the gibbets alongside. There are few historians or preservationists of power station plant but the outer walls of the West station are now incorporated into a classy apartment block.

To develop my career, I moved subsequently to Meopham (on the LC&DR) and then in 1972 into Great Western and Midland territory in Gloucestershire. Since taking early retirement in 1992, my creative energy has been devoted largely to railway interests with a steady output of books, articles, talks and model railways. Although firmly entrenched in the Cotswolds, I retain fond memories of suburban Lewisham and its railway connections.

This article is dedicated to my mother for rescuing her family from the ravages of war. You read this by courtesy of her gallantry and by the chance of our survival - a roll of the dice.

The Mystery Platforms (south of the flyover)   *Photo by Horace Tonge*

This scene of the 1957 St Johns accident appears to show an outer platform on the far side and a disused island platform between the centre tracks. The near face of the latter has been cut away but there are edging flags visible on the far face and the stub of a lamp-post in the middle. However, upon closer examination of this and other photographs, it transpires that these observations are an illusion. The correct identification is as follows:
  - The 'outer platform' on the far side is the top of lock-up garages behind Elswick Road.
  - The 'island platform' is the floor of the leading coach of the damaged Ramsgate train.
  - The 'edging flags' of the latter are floor coverings of the side corridor.
  - The 'stub of a lamp-post' is a brake wheel support column in the guard's compartment.
  - The four black cylinders at the far end are steam heaters under the seats.

The leading coach was a BR Mark 1 second class corridor brake built in 1956. It narrowly escaped being crushed by the falling bridge but its chassis was distorted beyond repair. It was cut up on site, together with the second coach and most of the flyover. Reference 6 gives a comprehensive account of the accident and rebuilding.

The St Johns Accident of 4 December 1957

Four photographs from the collection of John Hatherell, a former civil engineer of BR Southern Region who worked on the bridge rebuilding:

Opposite top - *The flyover after the accident, photographed from where the leading coach of the Holborn train leant dangerously into the decline. The truss on the left was later repaired and remains in service to this day.*

Opposite bottom - *The collapsed bridge was jacked up to facilitate safe cutting up for removal. A small army of railwaymen worked on the rescue, demolition and rebuilding. St John's church is top left.*

Top right - *When an irresistible force meets an immovable object, something has to give. In this case, the EMU coach has buckled and sheared beyond repair but the locomotive's bogie truck remains on the rails. The locomotive was subsequently repaired - Battle of Britain class Pacific No. 34066* Spitfire.

Bottom - *With demolition completed, work has started on the foundations of the new 'temporary' trestle bridge support. The North Kent line to Lewisham reopened the day after the accident, seen here with a Down freight train. All lines reopened within six weeks.*

References
1. Coulter, John, *Lewisham History and Guide*, Alan Sutton Publishing, 1994.
2. Bannerman, Lucy, *50 Years On...*, a report on page 26 of The Times newspaper, 3 December 2007.
3. Marshall, C.F.Dendy, revised by Kidner, R.W., *History of the Southern Railway*, Ian Allan, 1964.
4. Hatton, Graham, *Permanent Way Notes - Lewisham 1949*, The Southern Way, Preview Issue, Kevin Robertson (Noodle Books) 2007.
5. Mitchell, Vic and Smith, Keith in association with Leslie and Philip Davis, *London Suburban Railways - Holborn Viaduct to Lewisham including the Greenwich Park branch*, Middleton Press, 1990.
6. Tatlow, Peter, *St John's Lewisham 50 Years On*, The Oakwood Press, 2007.
7. Mitchell, Vic and Smith, Keith, *Southern Main Lines - Charing Cross to Orpington*, Middleton Press, 1991.
8. Mitchell, Vic and Smith, Keith, *London Suburban Railways - London Bridge to Addiscombe*, Middleton press, 1993.
9. Turner, Simon T., *Crystal Palace District Gas 1870-1914*, Issue 53, Archive, Lightmore Press.

EXPELLED!

The success of the 'Schools' class both as reliable machines and likewise over the choice of names is well known. Indeed their persona in the eyes of the public relative to the choice of names for the class, is, according to Bradley, down to a suggestion made by the Chief Draughtsman at Eastleigh that the names of public schools both within and beyond Southern territory be used. With a second batch of 20 engines ordered in March 1931 so the namings continued, and all went well, that is until No 923 was named 'Uppingham' in December 1933. Indeed it had been the practice for the newly christened locomotive to be exhibited at the nearest station to the actual school, that is assuming the school in question was on Southern territory, hardly appropriate in the case of Uppingham as the location this time is in Rutland.

Up to this now too, there appears to have not been a single murmur of discontent over the selection, that is until the Uppingham Headmaster J F Wolfenden heard of the naming, perhaps best described by Bryan Matthews in his 1984 book 'By God's Grace, a History of Uppingham School'*. (J F Wolfenden had taken over as Headmaster in March 1934, replacing R H Owen, a stern direct man described as a "martinet" and "strict disciplinarian" who had been in place between 1916 and 1934.) "He (Wolfenden) was very conscious, as he told the school on the first occasion it was assembled before him, that he was succeeding a Headmaster with a great reputation; in one or two instances in fact during his first years be seemed to out-Owen Owen........He was also very conscious of Owen's dislike of advertising, and in his first term wrote to the Southern Railway to complain that they had named one of their 'Schools Class' locomotives 'Uppingham' without leave. The directors of the company were astonished that any school should react like this, having imagined that all would feel honoured to have their names so displayed, but they met his wishes and renamed the engine ' Bradfield'. One of the offending plates was acquired by a member of the School years later and hangs in the Thring Centre'.

And there matters might have rested, that is until a regular contributor and friend of *Southern Way* suggested I might like to look in his garage....there hanging on the wall was the second plate, acquired as far back as 1966 having been similarly forgotten for the past decades. The rest as they say, is history.

(Contributed with grateful thanks).
* 'By Gods' Grace, a History of Uppingham School', by Bryan Matthews. Published by Whitehall Press, 1984.

LIFE AT SOUTHAMPTON TSO
Richard Simmons

Part 2: Specific Routes and Traffic Flows

Continuing on with this very popular series on life at the Southampton Train Supervisors Office, 'Control', from the mid 1950s onwards.

The first instalment appeared in Issue 6 of 'Southern Way'. More will follow shortly.

The Interlopers.

"Foreign" locomotives from other regions also worked into the district. From the WR there were regular workings (usually 'Halls') throughout the year, so enabling crews to retain route knowledge which might be needed especially for additional summer Saturday workings. One of these turns was the 9.10 am Reading - Portsmouth & Southsea returning at 3.45 pm. Another was the 6.50 am Reading - Southampton Terminus and corresponding 10.13 return. Following revision of the fish train (to be described in a continuing article), a 'Hall' worked the 10.23 am York - Bournemouth West from Banbury, returning to Reading from Bournemouth Central on the 7.48 pm Weymouth – Reading, but if my memory

is correct, the York train was crewed south of Oxford by SR men. WR locomotives, usually '2251' 0-6-0s regularly worked to Southampton Terminus from Didcot on DN&SR trains and in the late 1950s, was memorable by the 12.42 pm Didcot-Southampton Terminus and 4.56 pm return being hauled quite often by the celebrated 4-4-0 'City of Truro'. I took a photograph at St. Denys to prove it. From the former Midland and South Western Junction Railway direction came '43XX's. One arrived on the 4.10 am Cheltenham High Street - Southampton Old Docks freight (conveying beer from the Burton-on-Trent breweries to Southampton), then ran light to Bevois Park sidings (in later years renamed Southampton up yard) taking empty wagons as required to Washwood Heath. Another worked the 1.56 pm Cheltenham Spa (Lansdown)

41329 shunting the terminus of the freight only Bishops Waltham branch from Botley on a frosty 18th December 1961.

'M7' 30056 between Branksome and Parkstone with the 4.34 pm Bournemouth West - Brockenhurst (Old-Road) service comprising pull-push fitted stock, 18th August 1962.

- Southampton Terminus going home on the 7.04 pm Southampton Old Docks - Cheltenham High Street freight. There was also a regular turn for a 'Manor' on this route, generally 7818 'Granville Manor' or 7815 'Fritwell Manor', which had an out and back working on the 10.10 am Cheltenham Spa (Lansdown) - Southampton Terminus returning at 4.36 pm. The LMR was only represented in the Poole / Bournemouth area and on S & D trains. Obviously a number of these diagrams were amended as the years progressed.

Pull and Push (P&P) Trains

Such trains worked on the following lines and branches, but this method of operation did not necessarily apply to all services;- Eastleigh - Alton (Mid-Hants line), Fareham - Alton (Meon Valley line), Fareham - Gosport, 'Old Road' services (Brockenhurst - Bournemouth West via Ringwood) and Lymington and Swanage branches. They were originally shown in WTTs with a star at the head of the column and a general note that they were push and pull trains. By 1955 such workings had been redesignated 'Rail Motor' no doubt by BR dictum. These trains were usually formed of two coaches of pre-grouping stock, pulled or propelled by an 'M7' 0-4-4T. At the driving end, this stock had four rather deep windows, two

either side of the centre line thus presenting a reasonable appearance. Circa 1960, some Maunsell corridor stock was converted to P & P operation with driving end windows of a smaller size but standard with that then being fitted to new EMU stock built in the same era. The main visual difference was that whilst the EMUs had apertures between these windows for a numerical headcode, P & P sets didn't and so presented a rather blank 'slab end' look.

P & P trains were strengthened in time of need by 'air controlled seconds', signifying that such coaches were Westinghouse brake fitted and capable of being incorporated into P & P workings. Also on 'Old Road' services, some trains also conveyed an air-controlled PMV. This must have been unique on P & P trains but was necessary for two principal reasons. Firstly, no separate parcels trains ran over this route, so such traffic for the then small towns and hinterland of Wimborne and Ringwood had to be conveyed by these ordinary services. Thus after the line closed, for a short time a van train ran from Poole to Ringwood and return. Secondly was the pram traffic from Creekmoor Halt to Poole. Creekmoor, on the Poole outskirts, was already developing and wives with small children required to travel to Poole and back for shopping etc. It has to be remembered that in the late 1950s and early 1960s not so many traditional families had a family car and if they did, it was only one. Furthermore, at this time the folding baby buggy, so familiar today was unknown, prams being of the four wheeled rigid frame variety which could not be conveyed on buses, so the train was the only means of conveyance.

The Sectional Appendix permitted certain trains on the Lymington and Swanage branches to be worked without a guard provided that the number of coaches on such trains did not exceed three and were composed entirely of vehicles fitted with the vacuum brake. Trains requiring guards were generally confined to the Swanage branch, which conveyed through portions to and from Waterloo as well as the P& P set, the guard here being a member of the Porter / Guard grade. Passenger services on both the Gosport branch and Meon Valley line were discontinued from 8th June 1953 and 7th February 1955 respectively so were pre-Beeching closures and had gone by the time I returned from National Service. Motive power and rolling stock for the Mid-Hants line were

provided from Eastleigh's resources.

The Lymington branch engine was shown in the engine workings as being a Lymington duty but was supplied by Eastleigh. It slumbered overnight in the small sub-shed at Lymington Town and if, at around 5.30 am, a seemingly distant voice came on the phone from Lymington Town to say that the driver or fireman had not signed on duty, local staff had to be called out to organise taxis for passengers until Eastleigh MPD could find and get a replacement crew member to Lymington. Eastleigh loco was also responsible for supplying necessary oil. It seemed all too frequently, although it probably wasn't, that the Lymington driver was complaining that the oil cans had not arrived and the amount of oil available to him was steadily diminishing. We would connect him by phone straight to Eastleigh MPD to organise supplies. When the Lymington branch locomotive was due for changeover, Eastleigh loco advised the TSO who in turn advised Eastleigh West box that the loco would appear at

82028 arriving at Ringwood with the 12.08 pm Brockenhurst - Bournemouth West service, 28th March 1964. Despite the seeming hive of activity, the 'old-road' was closed as a through route just six weeks later.

the depot exit and it was then allowed on to the main line to run to Brockenhurst for change-over. Additionally the signal boxes along the route and the Lymington branch driver all needed to be informed. The branch P & P set inter-worked with 'Old Road' services and so reached Bournemouth West depot for change-over when necessary etc.

'Old Road' and Swanage branch engines and rolling stock were provided by Bournemouth, the job of changing over on the Swanage branch being made easy by the fact that there were at least two through workings to or from Bournemouth Central or Bournemouth West.

Castle Cary - Weymouth.

As this line was worked fully under WR regulations, we had to acquaint ourselves with the train classification as used by all other regions, the SR at that time not having adopted it. Clear instructions existed for banking arrangements up Evershot bank but on Bincombe bank WR and SR methods differed. The WR were quite happy for their trains to pull out of Weymouth station, stop at Weymouth Junction, even though this meant losing approximately three minutes for the banking engine to buffer-up, but not couple to the rear and bank as far as Bincombe Tunnel box. Here the banker would drop off, reverse into the refuge siding - which was an elongated crossover between up and down lines - and await a pathway to return to Weymouth.

Conversely, SR trains requiring assistance, were booked an assisting engine, coupled at the front before departure from Weymouth station. This would then assist through to Dorchester South and uncouple during the regular slick reversing movement back into the up platform thereby not losing time. No doubt this arrangement was inspired by strict timekeeping measures initiated by a former Southern Railway Superintendent of Operation. When the SR gained full responsibility for compiling Weymouth - Castle Cary WTTs, all WR trains requiring assistance were booked three minutes at Weymouth Junction for the banker to come on to the rear of trains. A WR engine though could not assist an SR engine, as the former worked on 25 inches of vacuum and the latter 21 inches. On the odd occasion when the only way of providing banking for an SR train to Bincombe was by stopping at Weymouth Junction for a banker so losing three or so minutes in the process; the CTC was most unhappy! Similar time allowance for a banker up Evershot bank was included in WTTs by the SR. Due to the aforementioned difference in vacuum created by WR and SR engines, a further complication arose in that an ex-WR and SR locomotive could not be coupled together. When a banked train was booked to call at Upwey and Broadway, the banking locomotive at the rear had to be coupled to that station, uncouple there and afterwards continue banking loose to Bincombe Tunnel box. The Sectional Appendix also included instructions for when it

Formerly operated mainly with pull-push passenger workings, in 1959 the Meon Valley route had already been closed for four years although from Fareham it was still open as far as Droxford for freight. Here a Branch line Society special is seen leaving Droxford heading back towards Fareham with 'M7' 30111 in charge. 7th March 1959. (The service had first arrived in the area at Portsmouth and visited the Bishops Waltham and Gosport lines on the same day. A maximum 20 mph speed limit was specified on the various branch lines with all points being clipped and 'plugged' as necessary.

was necessary to use three engines from Weymouth, but I have no recollection of such instances coming about.

Bridport branch trains used a bay on the up side at Maiden Newton and when steam reigned supreme, upon arrival the engine pushed the stock, usually a WR 'B' set, back into an inclined siding. After the engine had been removed the stock was gravitated back into the bay platform. This movement was applied with precision, as I never knew of the stock overshooting the stop blocks. Passenger services over the extension from Bridport to West Bay were withdrawn as long ago as 1930, but a 'Q' freight trip was timetabled until withdrawn from 3rd December 1962. After dieselization, a freight departed from Maiden Newton for Bridport at 6.18 am but curiously returned at 7.30 am as a mixed train. Later in the afternoon a light engine went to Bridport to work the 6.55 pm freight to Maiden Newton. However, with withdrawal of the West Bay 'Q' trip this train was retimed to start much earlier at 9.40 am.

Bristol - Weymouth services, together with the Bridport branch, became DMU operated to an enhanced timetable from 15th June 1959 but some steam-hauled trains remained, especially on summer Saturdays. Freight traffic continued to be handled on the short truncated stub of the Abbotsbury branch as far as Upwey Goods (formerly Upwey) and to Portland and Easton, although I recall one 'Royal' special ran from Portland. The terminus of the latter branch at Weymouth was Melcombe Regis, a short distance from the main station. Melcombe Regis closed at the cessation of passenger services to Portland and Easton but handled DEMU operated stopping trains from Eastleigh on summer Saturdays in 1958 and 1959.

Banking Arrangements

Having considered Bincombe and Evershot, the other two 'banks' worthy of mention are Parkstone and on the Romsey-Andover Junction line from Fullerton to Andover Junction. To Parkstone first. Here the 'bank' extended from between Poole and Parkstone up to Branksome. The Western Sectional Appendix decreed that all trains in either direction must stop at Poole station. I have never been able to discover why this came about, but the instruction was rescinded in later years. Freight trains leaving Poole yard seemed to be exempt from this stop, maybe it was deemed that they had stopped before they started. However, the close proximity of a level crossing, now replaced by a road overbridge at the London end of the station, prevented an assisting engine being coupled to the front of trains, as was the case for SR trains at Weymouth. In those days, the majority of Waterloo-bound trains from Weymouth were formed of no more than about four or five coaches, the 6-dining set having formed the Bournemouth West portion which was attached at Bournemouth Central and so were quite within the capability of the train engine for which the maximum tonnage for the various locomotive classes, unassisted, were shown in the Sectional Appendix.

On summer Saturdays, however, trains of about ten coaches came from Weymouth and so were rostered for banking assistance from Poole to Branksome. Trains were banked from the rear and in clear weather and provided Branksome box was open, which it usually was, and the train not booked to call at Parkstone or Branksome, the banking engine need not be coupled and ceased banking at Branksome. When a train was scheduled to call at Parkstone and not Branksome, the banker had to be coupled to the train as far as Parkstone and uncouple there. If calling at both stations, it would run coupled to Branksome; uncoupling was done by the fireman. Should Branksome box be closed, or during fog or falling snow, the banking engine had to be coupled and run through to Bournemouth Central. In practice, S & D crews, after pounding over the Mendip banks, did not usually require any banking assistance.

Occasions did arise when an up SR train from Weymouth, although not booked to be assisted did require assistance, in which case the footplate crew would advise the station staff at Dorchester South who passed the message on to the TSO who in turn arranged with Poole. It was then that the Poole yard shunter would normally be used.

Banking between Fullerton and Andover Junction

was rare because few freight trains traversed the line. The heaviest freights were the 7.04 pm Southampton Old Docks-Cheltenham (High Street), plus the occasional banana train. Should a banker be required, the TSO was advised probably before the train left its starting station and Andover Junction MPD advised. There were particular instructions as to when a WR or SR locomotive should be used.

Eastleigh

This was one of the district 'hubs', with the east and marshalling yards being the two principal sorting sidings for freight. Basically, east yard dealt with down traffic, arriving at the north end and controlled by Allbrook box. Departing traffic exited at East Junction box at the London end of the station. Marshalling yard dealt with all traffic to and from the Chandlers Ford and Botley lines, together with all up traffic from the Southampton direction. When considered now, the method of entering marshalling yard from the Southampton direction was horrendous. Trains had to pass through the station and on to No.1 up goods, a line parallel with the up slow between East Jct. and Allbrook - with an exit at the latter box. Here the train came to a stand, clear of East Junction, but then proceeded to reverse across all four running lines and back into the yard. All this with loose coupled wagons and in darkness controlled by paraffin lit shunt signals supplemented by the Guard's paraffin hand lamp. Even so I do not recall any derailments arising from this move, thus typifying train crew professionalism.

Also located at Eastleigh were the well-known locomotive and carriage works and large running shed. With an engine freshly ex-works and requiring a short 'run in' to bed down, the latter establishment often requested the TSO to grant a pathway for a light engine run from Eastleigh to Botley and back. Both works had their fortnights annual leave at the same time, for which on the first Saturday morning a special train was provided. For some reason the authorities considered most wanted to spend their holiday in the west country and the usual destination was Plymouth Friary.

Quite extensive carriage sidings also existed at Eastleigh, and a request for a special empty van train to Clapham Jct. was not uncommon from the passenger rolling stock department.

Signalling, Equipment Failures

All these had to be recorded in the daily log. The signal or point number together with description, e.g. up-home or when points were involved, down-to-up crossover etc, had to be noted, together with the failure time, the time the lineman was called, time of arrival, rectification time and delays arising from the failure. In cases of single line tablet failure, details of time and trains involved plus

Between Southampton Central and Millbrook, 30th April 1958. A defective point motor allowed a set of point blades to open just as 73111 was approaching on the 12.02 pm Southampton Central - Bournemouth Central stopper. The Eastleigh crane, DS35, is in attendance.

setting up and withdrawal of pilot working were required plus details of the train with which normal working was resumed.

Engineering Works.

These were most certainly not on the scale of today's activities and complete line closures on bank holidays were unheard of. All of this department's trains were loosely referred to as 'ballast trains', whose timings, formations plus the section of line scheduled to be under engineer's possession were given in the special traffic notices. What had to be watched was whether the possession would overrun and if so, we would arrange consequential service alterations.

Mishaps.

Fortunately during my time in the TSO, these were principally confined to wagon derailments in yards and so clear of the main running lines. Station Masters or yard staff were responsible for calling out the breakdown cranes, or 'heavy lifters' as they were generally known, from the MPDs. Again, details had to be recorded in the daily log which included the type of wagon and number, how many wheels were derailed, the time of the derailment, when the heavy lifters were called, their time of arrival, re-railment time and departure time of crane. Details of any track damage had also to be noted. When passenger vehicles were involved, coach type and number and set number were also needed.

There was one derailment, however, of which I took the first message. This was on 30th April 1958 when Standard 'Class 5' No 73111 and leading coach of the 12.02 pm Southampton Central - Bournemouth Central, became derailed between Southampton Central and Millbrook fortunately without injuries.

Weather Forecasts.

These were received from the RAF meteorological office at Upavon on Salisbury Plain, and were confined to fog, frost and snow warnings. Details were phoned to key stations, the CCE and S&T departments so that the necessary precautions as existed at the time could be taken.

'Circular 20'.

This was an early form of passenger information system which would nowadays be considered primitive. Telephone advice was received of any passenger service interruption to SR service and sometimes of major delays on other regions. The TSO then advised major stations, who in turn advised smaller stations in their locality. The term 'Circular 20' was derived from the circular number setting out instructions.

Returning now to more normal workings, let us consider some major traffic flows and firstly, scholars. There were a number of boarding schools, principally in the Bournemouth, (which was in Hampshire in those days) and south Dorset area, whose pupils mostly arrived and departed by train at the beginning and end of term. This was referred to as 'schools vacation traffic' and usually

With an SR pilotman on board, 'B1' No. 61119 is recorded passing Botley on Wednesday 6th May 1959 en route from Portsmouth via Botley, Eastleigh, Basingstoke and Clapham Junction to Leyton (Midland Road) where arrived was scheduled for 9.38 pm. The down direction journey had seen the 'B1' traverse the Portsmouth direct route via Guildford. Two educational excursions had run that day, the second being from Waterloo to Southampton Docks, which returned to Waterloo in a 'Q' path from the Docks some 40 minutes ahead of the 'B1'.

required special trains to and from Waterloo. In those days too, the general education system was different to the present day and may perhaps can be considered as being somewhat parochial. In Hampshire there were three County Boroughs, equal to today's unitary authorities, these were Portsmouth, Southampton and Bournemouth and which were completely separate from county council administration and so ran their own schools. Thus children resident in the county boroughs could not attend county council run schools and vice versa. Secondary or Grammar schools in the county were located at such places as Eastleigh and Brockenhurst, resulting in a considerable number of scholars travelling by ordinary train services to reach their places of education. But such were the number in some areas, that special unadvertised scholars trains were required. I recall three, 8.08 am Christchurch - Brockenhurst returning at 4.15 pm, 8.30 am Lymington Town - Brockenhurst returning at 4.01 pm and 8.25 am Totton - Eastleigh returning at 4.18 pm. For some time in its career, the Totton train was noteworthy by being formed of a Turnchapel or 'gate set' with iron gates controlling entry and exit. If such rolling stock was in service today I don't think health and safety people would be enamoured. The term 'Turnchapel sets' originated from the fact that they once worked that branch. The

Turnchapel sets were also equipped for pull and push working but did not work in that mode on the Totton trains. Quite a number of pupils were conveyed to Brockenhurst from such stations as Ringwood on the 6.35 am Weymouth - Brockenhurst via Broadstone and Ringwood, which went through a period of poor timekeeping for reasons I can no longer recall. But I do remember that the school headmaster was soon on the phone to the Chief Trains Clerk (CTC) on the occasions the train was late, so the TSO had to keep a careful check on the train's progress so the CTC could be pre-advised as to when it was late and why!

Educational excursions

These were also a summer feature, Southampton Docks and Portsmouth Harbour being favourite destinations. A not unusual itinerary was, train to Southampton Terminus, cruise down Southampton Water to Portsmouth and return from there or vice versa. Quite often such trains brought unusual locomotives into the area, and I have a photograph of 'B1' 4-6-0 61119 passing Botley on the 6.03 pm Portsmouth Harbour - Leyton (Midland Road) on 6th May 1959. Allowing for the time taken for this train to traverse the numerous London

Type '2' diesel-electric locos D5004 and D5013 passing Sholing just before mid-day on Friday 17th July 1959 with empty stock of a an educational excursion. Leaning out of the rear cab of D5004 is Eastleigh diesel fitter Les Elsey, no doubt present as a form of insurance for what was unusual motive power. The train had departed from Lewisham at 8.06 am running first to Clapham Junction and then down the main line to its destination at Southampton Terminus. This was no doubt an occasion when the party on board made their way to Portsmouth by water, as the stock was scheduled to leave ECS from Southampton Terminus at 11.35 am and then berth at Fratton at 12.28 pm. The return from Portsmouth was at 6.30 pm, travelling via Fareham, Botley, Eastleigh, Basingstoke and Clapham Junction to arrive back at Lewisham at 9.24 pm. Unusually, the special notice for the working clearly indicates 'South Eastern Division Diesel Engine' for the down working and ECS turns, but this is not mentioned for the return. Probably a simple oversight.

junctions to reach its final destination, one wonders what time these youngsters reached home for bed that evening. Another interesting working occurred on 17th Jury 1959, when D5004 and D5013 together worked an educational excursion, later the 11.35 am ECS Southampton Terminus - Fratton.

Southampton Docks.

The foundation stone for the docks was laid in October 1838 by a private company, appropriately named the Southampton Dock Company, but became railway owned when purchased by the LSWR in November 1892. Originally comprising only one set of docks at the confluence of the Rivers Test and Itchen, the facilities were expanded on the north bank of the River Test from the late 1920s by the Southern Railway. On the opposite bank of the river to these docks is Dibden Bay where in recent years Associated British Ports (ABP) sought planning permission to construct additional container berths but consent was not given. One can only wonder if the SR experienced similar difficulties with the appropriate authorities with their plans for docks expansion. The present situation is that there are now two entirely separate sets of docks, the original being named the Old Docks and those constructed by the SR in the 1920s etc, the New Docks. The 1962 Transport Act abolished the British Transport Commission and established the British Transport Docks Board, thus divorcing docks from railway management. The docks are now owned by ABP. 1965 saw new names applied. Old and New docks becoming Eastern and Western respectively.

The Old docks abounded with sharp radius curves, requiring short wheelbase shunting locomotives, hence the Adams 'B4' 0-4-0Ts which were superseded from about 1946 by 'USA' 0-6-0Ts redundant following cessation of World War II hostilities. In sharp contrast to the Old docks, the New docks was constructed with more or less straight lines and whilst the smaller shunting engines worked here, it was also home for longer wheelbase 0-6-0Ts of the LBSCR 'E1' and 'E2' classes. From 1962 steam traction was gradually replaced by Ruston & Hornsby CL.07' 0-6-0 diesel shunters. There was a small MPD in the Old docks where shunting locomotives were allocated and serviced, but this shed took no part in providing and servicing main line locomotives for passenger and freight trains which always came from and returned to Eastleigh MPD.

Connecting the 'outside world' to the Old docks, was a two line level crossing across the public Canute Road, adjacent to Southampton Terminus station and controlled by Canute Road ground frame. A few hundred yards away was a single line level crossing leading to the Channel Islands berths and shed. Neither crossing was gate-protected, but hand-signalmen halted road traffic by means of flags and hand bell. I have often wondered what became of that bell. Entrance and exit at the New docks boasted nothing so exciting as men with flags and bells, being a conventional double line connection with the main line near Millbrook station.

There was a means of transfer for rail traffic between both dock estates, by means of what was known as the Harbour Board lines, for which the sectional appendix detailed special working instructions - as it did for working in the docks in general. The Harbour Board lines ran alongside several busy roads and crossed the busy access road to the Town Quay, which, because of even sharper radius curves, was shunted by one of the diminutive Drummond 'C14' 0-4-0Ts until replaced by a Drewry diesel in the early 1960s. Ships berthing at the Town Quay were generally coastal freight vessels especially to the Isle of Wight, this being before the advent of modern RO-RO ferries currently used. The Harbour Board lines were not signalled, movements being in charge of a pilotman. Various sidings diverged from these lines and on a cold, overcast day in January 1961, at one such siding adjacent to the Town Quay, Adams design 'T3' No 563, was loaded on to a road low loader for transportation to the former Clapham Museum. (See photograph in the first article in the is series, Page 45, 'Southern Way Issue 6').

Boat trains operated direct to both the Old and New docks but all freight traffic ran to or departed from the Old docks shunting ground, New docks traffic being tripped to the Old docks via the aforementioned Harbour Board lines. The TSO was not involved with internal docks movements, except for the fact that the Town Quay shunting locomotive was not stabled at the docks MPD and instead worked to and from Southampton Terminus MP sidings, being changed over by Eastleigh MPD as necessary. The TSO become involved in such changeovers as such movements required wide headways because of

the slow speed of the 'C14' class locomotive. Nevertheless, the TSO maintained close liaison with docks staff when dealing with traffic entering or leaving. Taking 1959/60 as an example freight train departures were as follows:

Departure Time	Destination
Weekdays	
00.01 MX	Eastleigh Marshalling Yard
01.20 SXQ	Nine Elms
02.10MO / 02.15 Q	Feltham
02.55 MXQ	Nine Elms
04.40 SXQ	Exeter Riverside via Chandlers Ford
10.22 SXQ	Woodford via DN&SR
11.25 SXQ	Temple Mills or WR via Basingstoke
11.55 SXQ	Salisbury Fisherton via Redbridge
12.33 MXQ	York via DN&SR
13.22 SX	Feltham
13.50 SXQ	Salisbury Fisherton via Redbridge
14.23 SXQ	Feltham
14.48 FSXO	Salisbury via Redbridge
15.55MSX/16.10 FO	Crewe via DN&SR
16.25	Feltham
17.50	Eastleigh Marshalling Yard
18.28 SXQ	Feltham
19.00 SX/19.12SXQ	Nine Elms
19.20	Birmingham via DN&SR
20.28 SO	Feltham
21.20 SX	Nine Elms
22.00 SX	Northam yd.
22.10 SXQ	Nine Elms
22.30	Woking
23.00	Nine Elms
Sundays	
12.43 Q	Crewe via Basingstoke
16.25 Q	Temple Mills via Basingstoke
17.35 Q	Crewe via Basingstoke
18.40	Cardiff via Redbridge
20.30 Q	Brighton via Netley & Havant
21.25	Nine Elms
21.40	Eastleigh Marshalling Yard
22.35	Nine Elms
23.00	Crewe via Basingstoke

Abattoirs

The district had two rail connected abattoirs, at Uddens, between West Moors and Wimborne on the 'Old Road', and at Funtley, on the single line between Knowle Junction and Fareham. (The railway always contrived to use the spelling 'Fontley'.) Both sidings were served in the down direction only with daily scheduled stops. Uddens was served by the (1957 timetable) 6.05 am Brockenhurst -Dorchester South and 7.37 am Salisbury west yard – Wimborne, and Funtley by the 8.15 am Eastleigh marshalling yard - Gosport and 9.35 am Eastleigh east yard -Fratton. There was also an if required 'Q' pathway, leaving Eastleigh marshalling yard at 2.00 pm for Fareham calling at Funtley. Even then there were very strict welfare regulations over the conveyance of cattle, all such wagons being advised forward, together with details of loading times and when the beasts had last been fed and watered.

Boat Trains.

My time in the TSO coincided with the heyday of the transatlantic ocean liner, providing numerous sailings across the Atlantic Ocean not only by the original 'Queen Elizabeth', 'Queen Mary' and other Cunard liners, but also by vessels from other English and foreign shipping lines. Liner turn-round times were often up to about five days duration - far different from today's slicker operations. The Union Castle line operated a regular weekly sailing to South Africa by its 'Castle' boats, known as the 'Cape' boats, leaving Southampton every Thursday at 4.00 pm with the inwards boat arriving approximately 6.00 am on Fridays. There were also cruise liners, services to Australia and troopships, the latter of the 'Empire' class, to mention a few, the latter conveying army personnel, both regular and national servicemen to world trouble spots policed by this country. Boat trains were numbered with a 'B' prefix starting at No. 1 on the first day of each month. Several were named, such as 'The Cunarder', 'The Holland American' and 'The Springbok' etc. For the Cunard 'Queen' liner, the last down train from Waterloo for liners traffic and also the first up train for incoming vessels, were formed exclusively or mostly of Pullman stock. Indeed, such were the number of boat trains, that the WTT included numerous 'Q' pathways timed in both directions between Waterloo and both set of docks.

Taking the 1958 WTT as an example, there were 26 down pathways and fourteen in the up direction. Why the imbalance I don't know. One down direction train ran regularly on Thursdays and one up on Fridays, supplemented as necessary, for South African boats. Forces personnel trains were also numbered, but in the 'F' series, having a prefix being the date of running and a serial suffix number.

Boats docking late, (Autumn fog or gales were the principal causes), necessitated TSO involvement to agree an alternative pathway with Woking TSO and also re-arranging the enginemen and guards' rosters. Woking had to agree the altered arrival time with Waterloo, where any arrival during the evening peak period was to be avoided if at all practicable. When agreement had been reached with all concerned, signal boxes had to be advised. Vans conveying passengers' luggage always were marshalled next to the engine on up trains, so that upon arrival at Waterloo, luggage could be unloaded near to the barrier. As it became more plentiful, boat train sets were formed of Mark 1 stock, known as the '350' sets, but formations did vary according to boat loadings plus the addition of Pullman cars as necessary.

Train	From	To	Alteration or Provision	
a.m. 8 54	Waterloo	Southampton Docks (Train No. B.50—'Iberia')	1 C.P.M.V. * 1 B.S.K. * 2 S.O. * 1 F.K. 3 F.K. 1 Pullman buffet car— * 3 S.O. * 1 B.S.K.	*—352 set
9 30	Waterloo	Southampton Docks (Train No. B.52—'Chusan')	1 C.P.M.V. * 1 B.S.K. * 2 S.O. * 1 F.K. 3 F.K. 1 Pullman buffet car * 3 S.O. * 1 B.S.K.	*—351 set
10 0	Waterloo	Southampton Docks (Train No. B.51—'Iberia)	1 C.P.M.V. * 1 B.S.K. * 3 F.K. 1 F.K. 1 Pullman buffet car * 3 S.O. * 1 B.S.K.	*—353 set
10 22	Waterloo	Southampton Docks (Train No. B.53—'Chusan')	1 C.P.M.V. * 1 B.S.K. * 3 F.K. 1 Pullman buffet car * 3 S.O. * 1 B.S.K.	*—354 set

An example of just some of the boat train workings from Saturday 9th August 1958.

Away from the glamour of the main line, the goods on the truncated line from Fullerton Junction to Longparish, recorded below, at Wherwell, as the 8.45 am from Andover Junction, 25th May 1956 and the goods notice at the terminus.

Photographs by Richard Simmons.

TO BE CONTINUED

Above - *Some of the 25,000 toms of chalk which fell onto and across the railway on the evening of 28th November 1940. The occurrence had been detected by the signalman in Shakespeare Signal Box together with a watchman who was patrolling nearby.*

Left *- Track pushed aside with ease due to the force of the impact. In the background can be seen part of the new landmass on the former shoreline.*

'DÉ JÀ VU'

The 1939 Chalk Fall at Shakespeare Cliff

1939 was not a good year. Neither of course would be those that immediately followed, although the first year referred to in this piece had thrust the Southern Railway very much into the front line so far as the potential for defence and invasion were concerned. Here will not be the place where such issues are debated, suffice it to say that as resources were steadily being mobilised and prepared, so any homeland disruption was far from welcome.

But nature, perhaps even fate, might be considered to think otherwise, for in November 1939, just three months into what was fortunately still the 'phoney-war' period, a major landslip occurred destroying the line between Dover and Folkestone which was not even partially restored to traffic until January 1940. The phrase 'dé jà vu' is deliberately used in the heading to this piece, as at the height of WW1 in December 1915, a similar natural occurrence had taken place although on that occasion it rendered the railway closed until August 1919. (One other serious fall had occurred back in 1877 whilst there had been several lesser events in other years.)

Advances in science, particularly relative to soil mechanics, led to the discovery that the instability of the chalk in this area was due to geographical conditions, created by differing materials lying on top of each other and accentuated during periods of wet weather.

Knowledge in this area had been developed prior to 1939 but it was not until after 1948 that serious endeavours were made which, up to date, appear to have been successful. These new measures include drainage tunnels into the chalk, 'toe weighting' and increased protection against sea erosion.

Despite the secrecy that might have been expected to have been exercised at thus time, the *Railway Magazine* for October 1940 carried a major article on the recent slip, although it will be noted this was some months after the event and subsequent to the line being fully restored. Commencing with a précis of the history of the railway in the area and then describing in detail previous falls, the article goes on to refer to the 1939 situation as having its origins on the night of 28/29th November between the Abbotscliff and Shakespeare tunnels and on a stretch of line where, up to that time, no falls had ever been recorded, previous events having taken place at the Folkestone end of the line.

At the site of the 1939 slip, there had once existed what was a large isolated mount of chalk, known as Round Down Cliff which, during construction of the railway around 1843, was removed by blasting. The summit of the cliff here was some 375 feet above the high tide mark and 70 feet of cliff had to be removed over a distance of 300

Right - November 29th 1939, the morning after the night before. It is not reported exactly when clear-up operations began but it may be reasonable to assume this was sometime during the next day. The size of some of the boulders involved in the fall, reported as up to 10 tons in weight, can be seen.

The magnitude of the task is seen here when comparing the excavators with the size of the nearby boulders. The remains of the railway are visible in the background. The view is believed to have been taken around 21st December 1939.

feet. The demolished cliff fell alongside what was later the railway and subsequently became the site of Shakespeare Colliery.

Between the two tunnels, a distance of some two miles, the remaining cliff is up to 450 feet high, home it was stated at one time to a breeding herd of wild goats, reported as belonging to a local butcher, but which in the process of scrabbling up and down the face, were responsible for dislodging chalk. The animals were later shot by the RSPCA, either from the top of the cliff or from track level. It was these very cliffs which were often pictured in images accompanying the famous war time song, "There'll be bluebirds over the white cliffs of Dover". The railway was also protected by a sea wall between the tunnels.

Up to November 1939, the Southern had already commenced stabilising work in the are, leaving just some 200 yards more to be provided with a toe wall. Unfortunately the weather in the last quarter of 1939 proved to be unusually wet, October especially, with twice the rain of September and indeed almost half of what might reasonably be expected during a full year. A slip might thus be expected, but this was usually preceded by a smaller 'warning' slide. This was indeed the case, as on 27th November, some 50 tons fell from the cliff face fortunately without damaging the track. Even so the railway were prepared for worse, as close examination at the top revealed an open crack 8 inches wide and 20 feet from the face of the cliff. A continuous watch was kept and just 24 hours later, at 6.55 pm on 28th November, the signalman at Shakespeare 'box heard another fall occur

about 100 yards west of his cabin. He immediately stopped traffic by sending 'Obstruction Danger' and so halted the 5.00 pm from Canon Street at Folkestone Junction. This though was still just the beginning, as shortly afterwards what was later estimated to be some 25,000 cu.yds of material fell from the face, the amount of material completely swamping the railway, the site of the former colliery as well as forming additional land in the sea itself. Later estimates indicated the railway covered in chalk to a depth of about 20 feet over a distance of 80 yards and comprising in the main boulders estimated to weigh between 2 and 10 tons each.

The limited access available to the site meant that equipment and men had to be brought via the tunnels on either side and it was by this means that four excavators were summoned. Due to the actual tunnel clearance available, only a restricted size of excavator could be transported to the site, which were also unable to deal with any single boulder greater than around ¾ ton in weight. There was then considerable use of explosives and pneumatic hammers. Additionally, there were still areas of loose chalk on the face itself and these had to be removed by men, during daylight only, suspended by rope and harness 60 to 100 feet below the cliff edge.

Bus services, operated by the East Kent Road Car Co Ltd, maintained services between Folkestone and Dover whilst other trains, particularly the BEF Christmas Leave Trains, were diverted over the boat train route running via Chatham.

Partial reopening of the line took place on 7th January, but the still soaked chalk, aggravated by front and

THE 1939 CHALK FALL AT SHAKESPEARE CLIFF

Top - *Nature in full force. Years earlier it had been believed that is was simple erosion at the base of the cliff that created the conditions for a fall, hence the provision of the sea defences. Whilst these were undoubtedly useful, it was only later that it was realised other factors, particularly weight and drainage, played just an important a role.*

Middle - *So far as the SR was concerned, the stretch of line between Dover and Folkestone was stated to be that which was the most costly to maintain. One contemporary commentator going further by stating it was the most expensive within the country. This would conveniently ignore the other obvious exposed location around Dawlish.*

Bottom - *Here work is going on with both excavators and draglines, the equipment hired from outside contractors. Whether is was just contract labour that was involved is not reported.*

snow, resulted in further sporadic falls. To clear this new debris, another period of closure was necessary from the evening of 5th February until 8th February. Afterwards trains were only permitted during daylight hours, with an inspection made every morning prior to traffic.

These precautions were wisely made, as just over two weeks later on 23rd February, another estimated 10,000 tons of loam and chalk fell some 70 yards from the Dover portal of the tunnel destroying the railway and the sea wall at this point. Another 1,000 tons fell at a point between Martello Tunnel and the Warren Halt at 11.00 am the same day. Again this last fall was just a warning, as over the next 24 hours what was estimated at a further 100,000 tons fell from the cliff. Fortunately here the cliff face was some 250 yards back from the line, whilst a depression at this point also prevented any of the debris falling on to or over the track.. Even so the line was again

closed and remedial work undertaken, the heavy plant having remained on site at the Shakespeare sidings. Once more recourse was made to the 'bus company.

Traffic finally resumed again on 10th March, daytime services only, and with the line fully reopened on 21st April. Even so some remedial repairs were still being undertaken to the sea wall.

It was due to the history of events in the area that the Southern Railway had, in 1934, obtained an Act of Parliament for the construction of a new line inland. This would have involved leaving the existing route at Folkestone Junction and travelling then via a 3½ mile tunnel to rejoin the original route 500 yards west of the western entrance to Shakespeare Tunnel. Although marked out, no work was undertaken although in 1940 it was reported that an extension of time had been authorised.

Opposite and above - Seen on calm day and at low tide, it is hard to imagine the terrific forces involved. The views are all looking towards Dover. In later years 'toe-weighing', meaning adding solid stability to the very base of the cliffs at the point where they meet the sea below the railway, has increased the stability to the cliffs themselves. This is in the form of a concrete apron extending several hundred feet into the sea which was itself placed on a bed of Meldon rock and then covered with 43,000 tons of chalk.

Left - *Some impression of the size of the cliffs can be gauged from this ground level view: note the workmen and Wickham Trolley - visible with a telegraph pole seemingly attached to the body. It was on these cliffs that workmen were required to abseil, suspended from the top, to remove further potentially loose outcrops of chalk.*

Right hand page - *December into January 1939-1940. Much of the fallen material has by now been removed and efforts can be concentrated on preparing a foundation for a new line of rails. A limited service was restored, at reduced speed, from Sunday 7th January 1940, but it would be more than three months and after further curtailment, that services eventually returned to normal.*

Photographs from the RCHS - Spence Collection.

Nine of the 2,281 Locomotives inherited by the Southern Railway on the 1st January 1923 are lined up on what looks like Cannon Street Bridge. Just in front of the nearest loco, D class 4-4-0 No.740, the P' way department can be seen renewing timbers, suggesting this might be a weekend. The Locomotive next to No 740 is E class 4-4-0 No. 315 and the last one on the front row is another E class 4-4-0. On the far siding the front engine is a C class 0-6-0, the only other identifiable loco is E class 4-4-0 No. 275 which is standing behind the tender of No. 740. The photo was almost certainly taken in the years leading up to the First World War as all the locos except the C class are fully lined out and commendably clean, the C has just SE&CR on its tender.

The SOUTHERN RAILWAY:
from Inception, through to Nationalisation and beyond.
Part 2 - The Inheritance
Tony Goodyear

In the first article of this series we looked at what the Americans might call the "real estate" and liabilities that came with it, together with some of the colourful characters that ran the constituent companies before the grouping, a surprising number of them surviving to serve the newly formed Southern Railway with distinction. We also looked at the skills and knowledge that they passed on to the new organisation. In this article we will take a look at the fixed assets, electrification and track, together with the not-so-fixed assets, traction and rolling stock. Additionally we will look at the electrification systems that the Southern inherited, but it is the intention to deal with the development and implementation of the Southern's own electrification plans separately later in the series.

As we know, the Southern Railway's first day in business was the 1st of January 1923, and although much had been done towards this end, it was mostly at a local level and geared to ensuring the change-over was carried out as smoothly as possible. In practice things carried on much as before, with the main constituent companies' organisations largely continuing in place, receipts etc. being paid into new accounts. In the case of some of the smaller companies, particularly those on the IOW, a few staff were specifically retained to help produce final accounts and wind up the old companies. It was to be 7th June 1923 before the Southern board approved the main managerial appointments for the new organisation, the most important being that of Sir Herbert Walker as joint General Manager. Even then it took to the end of 1923 before Walker was able to submit to the Board an organisation for the management of the unified Southern Railway, which took effect in 1924. Following these formalities the old order finally started to disappear. It is clear from several sources that Herbert Walker went to some lengths to ensure that the new organisation was inclusive, and not seen as a complete takeover by the South Western men, particularly after having to ease out the other two joint General Managers, Sir William Forbes (LB&SC) and Percy Tempest (SE&CR).

On the 1st of January 1923 the Southern Railway inherited, according to C F Dendy Marshall, 2,178 miles 9 chains of route or first track, which comprised 4,175 miles 49 chains of running line and 1,205 miles 60 chains of sidings. There were 2,281 locomotives, 7,500 carriages (described as passenger-carrying vehicles) and 36,749 wagons. The accuracy of the figures quoted in Marshall's book has sometimes been called into question but I have used Dendy Marshall's figures as my main source of information for the early articles in this series for the following reasons: his book is the earliest full account of the setting up of the Southern Railway; it is clear that he was given full access to the records then held by the Southern Railway up to the time of the original publication in 1936, including those of the constituent companies; and the original edition was approved and published by The Southern Railway Company.

Unfortunately Dendy Marshall did not include a breakdown of the calculated combined mileage figure. Just adding together the mileages he quoted for the main constituent companies gives an answer that is somewhat short of his quoted figure. I have included a table of mileages Fig 1, overleaf, designed to show how the figures were arrived at. This has been compiled from a number of sources and includes, where possible, a little more detail than just the route mileage for each company.

The resulting table raises some interesting points. Of particular note is the low single track mileage of the SE&CR at just 65 miles (a shade over 10% of the total), see part 1 for the explanation of this. The LB&SCR at 100 miles, roughly 22% of the total and the comparatively large 324 miles of the South Western, which represented nearly a third of the route mileage at 32%, highlights the different priorities of the promoting companies at the time the various lines were originally built. Of the 553 miles of single track line inherited by the Southern Railway at the grouping, only 78 miles of it, is still in use as heavy rail line today (Croydon Tram Link track excluded). The other interesting point is that 30 miles (38.5%) of that figure is today operated by the various heritage railways.

Fig 1.Table of mileages for the operating constituent companies of the Southern Railway				
L&SWR	**Non Running Lines**	**Additional Running Lines**	**Running Line**	**Route Miles**
Route Miles				1019
Single Track			324	
Double Track			695	
Three Tracks		79		
Four Tracks		65		
Multiple Track		37		
Sidings	486			
LB&SCR				
Route Miles				457
Single Track			100	
Double Track			357	
Three Tracks		47		
Four Tracks		35		
Multiple Track		14		
Sidings	355			
SE&CR				
Route Miles				638
Single Track			65	
Double Track			573	
Three Tracks		40		
Four Tracks		29		
Multiple Track		23		
Sidings	348			
PD&SWJR				
Route Miles				9 54ch
Single Track			9.54	
IWR				
Route Miles				14
			14	
IWCR				
Route Miles				28 20ch
			28.20	
FYNR				
Route Miles				12
			12	
*Total Route Mileage				2177.74ch

*The total quoted by Dendy Marshall is 2178

The figures in the table reveal nothing about the state of affairs on the ground, which in more than a few cases was dire. All the three main constituent companies had suffered from nine years of restricted and poor maintenance due to government control during the war years (First World War or The Great War) and after. The Isle of Wight Companies were, for the most part, impoverished and had been able to do little more than essential maintenance for many years.

When we look back beyond the First World War, it is clear that the main constituent companies of the Southern had been making plans to upgrade and modernise their lines for some time. This was particularly true with respect to the London area operations as much traffic was being lost to the new electric tramways, which were in full expansion mode in the early years of the twentieth century. While in each case the ultimate solution was electrification, they all had different ideas about the method and how to achieve it.

The LB&SCR were first off the mark with their 6.6 KV AC overhead electrification of the South London Line from London Bridge to Victoria. The service was introduced on 1st December 1909 and known as the "Elevated Electric". Surprisingly, this was not the first AC overhead electric system in the UK. That honour fell to the Midland Railway when they opened their 9½ mile Morecombe, Lancaster and Heysham electrification scheme in 1908. The South London Line was soon followed by a scheme to electrify the lines from London

Bridge and Victoria (via Streatham Hill) to Crystal Palace, the first section of which opened for business on 22nd May 1911, the day King George V opened the "Festival of Empire" at the Crystal Palace. The section between Peckham Rye and Tulse Hill, enabling the service to London Bridge to be inaugurated, had to wait until 1st June 1912 to be energised as the power supply company had insufficient capacity. Work to electrify most of the remaining LB&SCR suburban network was authorised in 1913. Much work had been done, including erection of some of the overhead, before war was declared in August 1914 but as most of the electrical equipment was on order from German manufacturers, work stopped shortly after war broke out and was not resumed until just before the grouping, in 1922.

In the electrification stakes the L&SWR was next in the field; again it was the loss of traffic that prompted action. With the construction of the London United Tramways network and the electrification of the District Railway to Richmond and Wimbledon during 1906, followed by the opening of the Central and Piccadilly tube lines, it was obvious that something would have to be done to address the serious loss of traffic, which was stated to be the equivalent to 1.25 million passenger journeys per annum. The appointment of Herbert Walker as General Manager of the L&SWR in 1912 appears to have been the catalyst for progress. Following meetings with the supporters of the Central London Railway on their proposals to extend their line to Richmond and even beyond, powers for the Richmond extension being obtained in 1913, Walker reported his findings back to the board. The possibility of these railways expanding into their area through lack of foresight and action must have rattled the windows at Waterloo as later in 1913 the L&SWR announced comprehensive proposals for the electrification of their suburban lines.

Following the advice of the L&SWR's Electrical Engineer (Herbert Jones) and the consulting engineers Messrs Kennedy and Donkin, it was decided to adopt a 600v DC third rail system. The original ambitious 1913 scheme was intended to cover services on the lines from: Waterloo to Wimbledon via East Putney, the Waterloo to Waterloo roundabout services via Kingston and Hounslow, the Shepperton branch, Waterloo to Woking and Guildford via the main line, Waterloo to Guildford via Cobham (leaving the main line at Hampton Court Junction) and Waterloo to Guildford via Epsom (leaving the main line at Raynes Park). This scheme also provided for the erection of the L&SWR's own power generation plant (Power House) at Durnsford Road Wimbledon, together with their own 11 KV power distribution system, the conversion to 600v DC being carried out at local (rotary converter) sub-stations spaced out along the line, usually about 3 miles apart in the countryside.

Only the L&SWR electrification scheme was proceeded with after the outbreak of WW1. The L&SWR electrification was physically more advanced than the

others. The SE&CR scheme was only in the planning stage and the LB&SCR scheme relied heavily on foreign input (German). The L&SWR were very lucky to be allowed to continue work, albeit at a slower rate of progress but with Durnsford Road power house well advanced and much of the electrical equipment, for the early stages at least, on site or well in hand from British manufacturers, there would have been little point in leaving expensive equipment lying unused, no doubt a point forcibly argued by Herbert Walker at the time. It should be remembered that he was also acting chairman of the Railway Executive Committee, which took over control of the railways from the outbreak of war until the end of 1919.

The first L&SWR public electric trains ran between Waterloo and Wimbledon (via East Putney) on 25th October 1915, making use of the District line electrification of 1906 between East Putney and Wimbledon. The Kingston roundabout and the Shepperton branch services commenced on 30th January 1916, which was postponed from the advertised date of 5th December 1915, following objections from the Post Office, claiming that the new equipment caused interference with the operation of long distance telephone circuits. Services via the Hounslow loop were inaugurated on 12th March 1916 and those to Hampton Court were added on 18th June. The short section to Claygate, 3 miles from Surbiton down the Guildford (new Line) via Cobham line was brought in to use on 20th November 1916. This was as far as the L&SWR scheme got before it was halted by the war. In truth it had also probably run out materials by then. The sections from Raynes Park via Epsom and from Claygate to Guildford, which formed part of the proposed 1913 scheme, had to wait until after the grouping for their promised electric trains, the main line via Woking having to wait somewhat longer.

It was the SE&CR that ended up left out in the cold, when it came to getting a proposal off the ground for the electrification of the line. As early as 1903 the railway had obtained powers to work the line by electricity, which included a provision for the generation of electricity for the purpose, although nothing more was done at the time. Ten years later, with the successful LB&SCR electrification up and running, the Chairman, H. Cosmo Bonsor, told the proprietors at the half-yearly management meeting (probably after the L&SWR proposals were announced), that the "Managing Committee did not think it opportune to incur heavy capital expenditure to compete with trams and buses". All sorts of difficulties were put forward as to why it would be awkward and expensive to electrify the railway. Given that there were six London termini to deal with, a plethora of interworked services, many stations with short platforms to be extended and complicated junctions, there was some justification in being cautious. In practice the Management Committee were fully committed (financially) elsewhere and any spare monies that might have been available would have

Typical of the much of the turn of the century passenger stock inherited from the constituent companies is this South Eastern Railway six compartment Birdcage Brake third No 2294. It subsequently became SR No.3239 after the grouping.

been totally inadequate for the purpose. Any thoughts there may have been of progressing further with electrification at the time, were dashed by the outbreak of war in August 1914.

The pressing need to do something constructive to modernise the London suburban services did not go away, as it is clear that the SE&CR were working up a proposal for a comprehensive London area electrification programme to be introduced after the war. Many of the complications that existed before the war were for one reason or another removed because of it; examples being the cessation of services on the Greenwich Park branch and the withdrawal of services to Moorgate over the Metropolitan Extension, neither of which was resumed after the end of hostilities.

The scheme that developed was for a 1,500v DC side contact system using two conductor rails, with the live rail being fully protected. Once it was established that a government guarantee could be obtained, the SE&CR applied for permission from the Electricity Commissioners, under the powers obtained in 1903, to build their power station by the Thames at Angerstein Wharf, Charlton, in early 1922. Following a public inquiry, the application was refused on the grounds that the electricity should be obtained from an established electricity supply company. Clearly the company were unhappy with the decision and as their efforts to secure

electricity supplies continued to be unsuccessful, the SE&CR again approached the Electricity Commissioners stating that no satisfactory agreement could be arrived at. The Electricity Commissioners responded with a lengthy statement, which effectively pointed out that they considered the railway (probably any railway) as just another commercial customer and no different to a factory or steel works and it was up to them to establish a working relationship and appropriate rates with the supply company. As late as 13th December 1922, in connection with establishing the new constitution for the "Southern Railway" company, the SE&CR placed on record that they accepted the position of the Electricity Commissioners.

To all intents and purposes the SE&CR scheme ended there with the grouping less than a month away. It does beg the question though, as to why the SE&CR had the spat with the Electricity Commissioners, considering that the LB&SCR bought their electricity straight from a supply company. No doubt they remembered that the Brighton had to wait for over a year after the Victoria to Crystal Palace section was brought into use (May 1911 to June 1912), before the electricity company were in a position to provide enough power for the Peckham Rye to Herne Hill section of the Crystal Palace electrification. The other point to note is that both the District Railway and the L&SWR generated their own power and had their own power distribution networks; they were therefore, independent of the supply companies when it came to the security of supply. This point was not lost on the Southern management team and it must have been sorted out with the supply companies after the grouping as the Southern Railway established and maintained its own distribution and remote switching network, which enabled power to be drawn from alternative supply points, in the event of an interruption to supplies. This facility has been maintained and handed down through British Railways to Railtrack and is now in the hands of Network Rail.

As mentioned earlier, in the years before the grouping, the main constituent companies were also busy improving their infrastructure, often on the back of electrification schemes. The LB&SCR however, did little to enhance its infrastructure as a direct result of the electrification process, with activities mainly restricted to platform works and the provision of electrified sidings. It should be noted that the new sidings at Norwood were not accessible until after June 1912, when additional power supplies were made available. The Brighton did carry out a number of other improvement works such as the doubling of the line between Newhaven and Seaford and the quadrupling between Three Bridges and Balcombe Tunnel in the early years of the century. The quadrupling between Victoria and Windmill Bridge, Croydon; could loosely be considered as preliminary works for future electrification and was completed in 1907, together with the burrowing junctions at Windmill Bridge and Norwood.

All the upgrading works came to end after war was declared in 1914 and the LB&SCR found itself in the front line. Having two of the major ports of embarkation on its line, it was immediately faced with the problems of gearing up for the war effort. These activities initially stretched resources to the limit as the railway had to improve facilities at these ports quickly, with additional stabling sidings, power supplies and signalling not to mention the extra motive power and crews that also had to be found and provided. The two ports in question were Newhaven and the perhaps less obvious Littlehampton, which was added to the list of designated ports some months after the outbreak of war.

The L&SWR on the other hand, had carried out considerable additional works to upgrade their main line out of London, as part of its long standing policy of improvements to the infrastructure and the elimination of bottlenecks. Many sections of line were upgraded towards the end of the nineteenth century and in the early years of the twentieth century; the work usually being carried out in a series of individual stages, often over some years, so that as each section of line was completed, improvements in capacity and operation were achieved. In the London area efforts were concentrated on programmes for quadrupling the track and eliminating flat junctions by providing burrowing or flying junctions at strategic locations. The first of these was provided at Twickenham in 1882, taking the Up Kingston Loop Line over the Windsor Lines. On the main lines to Southampton and the

West Country the emphasis was on the completion of the four tracking to Basingstoke (Worting Junction) and the elimination of most of the flat junctions. To this end the section between Clapham Junction and Hampton Court Junction was completed on 5th November 1885. This included the provision of burrowing junctions at Raynes Park and New Malden in 1884. The remainder of the quadrupling and widening works, from Clapham Junction as far as Worting Junction, was finally completed in July 1905, leaving just a short section between Queens Road and Clapham Junction to complete the widening works through to Waterloo.

Following on from the initial four-tracking works, it was the remaining flat junctions on the main line that received the attention of the South Western's dedicated engineering teams. In the early years of the new century a burrowing junction was provided at Hampton Court Junction for the Up Guildford (New Line) in 1908. Later in 1915 a new separate down Hampton Court branch line from Surbiton together with a skew bridge over the main lines at Hampton Court Junction was provided in connection with the electrification of the Hampton Court branch. Other flat junctions were eliminated at Byfleet Junction in 1903 when the Down Chertsey Line was diverted under the main lines and in 1901 the Up Aldershot Line was carried over the main line at Pirbright Junction in preparation for quadrupling. Further down the line at Battledown the Up Southampton Line was realigned to pass over the West of England Lines in 1897, new signal boxes being provided at Battledown and Worting.

There were other engineering works of note including the provision of a third track between Grateley and Newton Tony, junction for the Amesbury branch. In November 1882, a third line was also brought into use, between Andover and Red Post Junction, to eliminate the original 'temporary' Red Post Junction, provided for the opening of the Swindon Marlborough and Andover Railway (SMA) (latter the M&SWJR), in March of that year. In future years two further junctions (on separate occasions) would be provided at this point and later eliminated again. Other improvement works, far too numerous to mention, were also carried out during this period but by far the most impressive was the completion of the long-drawn-out rebuilding of Waterloo station, which was formally opened by Queen Mary (deputising for the King who had a bad cold) on March 21 1922.

It could be said that work started in earnest on planning the new station, following a visit to the United States by J W Jacomb-Hood – Chief Engineer - and Sam Fay – Superintendent of the Line - in 1901, to study modern operating practices and terminal arrangements there. Planning the new station started soon after their return. Sam Fay moved on to the Great Central Railway as General Manager in March 1902, leaving Jacomb-Hood to carry on as best he could. The work was planned to progress from south to north commencing with the construction of the end wall alongside the new approach road, this section comprising platforms 1 to 11 coming into use in 1910. The modernisation had crept as far north as platforms 15 and 16 by 1919 when the escalator connection to the tube was brought into use. The office and amenities block (now demolished) between these two platforms, known to staff as 'the village block' was completed during 1920. The new entrance to the station in the north east corner was constructed in the form of a Victory Arch the left hand column of which is marked 1914 and is decorated with the Goddess of War, Bellona. The right hand column was marked 1918 and represented peace. When dedicated by the Queen in 1922 the names of the 585 L&SWR staff that died during the First World War were inscribed on bronze tablets.

As mentioned earlier the SE&CR were also on a mission to upgrade and improve their line. In part 1 mention was made of the particular legacy of poor construction on the South Eastern. This was particularly apparent in the state of the bridges and the right of way throughout the area covered by the old LC&DR and SER, which unlike the infrastructure of the L&SWR and the LB&SCR, had not been systematically upgraded over the years, due to the costly feuding and ruinous competition engaged in by these two companies, which left them almost destitute and unable to properly maintain their assets. The new management committee had much to do and very soon after taking office the board started to authorise upgrading work which amounted to a virtual reconstruction of much of the railway from the ground up. The work was overseen by Percy Tempest who had recently been appointed Chief Engineer. According to Dendy Marshall's account, the work consisted of the strengthening or renewal of 588 bridges and four tunnels (this probably included improving clearances as well), together with relaying the main lines with heaver rails and re-ballasting with Kentish stone.

Anxious to put the past behind them and to be seen to be doing the right thing, the managing committee gave an undertaking to Parliament in 1906 that: if 'The Dover Harbour Board enlarged the harbour' at Dover, they would within three years build a new marine station. Although the harbour and jetty had been built before war broke out, the new marine station was incomplete and work was halted. Once it was realised just how useful the station would be in repatriating the wounded, orders were given to complete the new station sufficiently to enable it to be used for the transfer of wounded solders between ship and train. The station was brought into use, for military purposes, during December 1914. Dendy Marshall states that 1,260,506 wounded were received at Dover; and despatched in 7,781 ambulance trains during the war period.

The SE&CR bore the full impact of the war on its operations in other ways too, for example, having to provide nearly 15,000 extra trains for forces leave during the four years of the conflict. In terms of volume that's about 10 trains a day, which accounted for the movement of just over 6.5 million men. In addition there were considerable quantities of military mail to be carried. Huge quantities of additional goods traffic had to be moved, with over a million wagon movements into and out of Woolwich Arsenal and the Royal Dockyard accounting for a further 452,000 movements. The creation of the new Port of Richborough just added to the pressure. Even though the managing committee had spent considerable sums on upgrading the line, the work was still far from complete. It was indeed fortunate that so much had been achieved but the truth was that the line could take nothing larger than a moderate sized 4-4-0 or 0-6-0, resulting in having to double head most trains to and from the channel ports; a very inefficient use of manpower and equipment at a crucial time.

Returning again to the inheritance theme, according to Dendy Marshall there were 2,281 locomotives passed to the Southern group on January 1 1923. Unfortunately this is an instance where various authors disagree over the totals. J H Russell's *A Pictorial Record of Southern Locomotives* quotes the total as 2,287, I have a problem with this number as it includes the four Lynton and Barnstaple engines which were not absorbed until after grouping took place but omits the three PD&SWJ engines which were. Russell does however, break down the total number into the contribution made by each of the constituent and absorbed companies, for details see my adjusted table Fig 2. opposite page. There was clearly a certain amount of licence used when deciding under which heading some locomotives should be declared, the figures though can be made to add up with a bit of juggling.

The locomotive stock contributed by each of the constituent companies very much reflected the traffic and operational mix that existed in each case.

The following sections take a fairly detailed look at what the Southern Railway inherited in the way of locomotive stock from all sources. The state of the locomotive stock at the grouping was crucial to the Southern's development plans.

For the most part the locomotives inherited from the South Western were a competent bunch by the time they were handed to the Southern. A few even had origins dating back to the 1870s and the days of Beattie Snr., the three well-tanks at Wadebridge surviving nearly another forty years into the late BR steam era. There were also a fair number of Beattie Jnr's., engines still on the books at this time but it was the Adams, Drummond and Urie engines that were shouldering the burden on a daily basis. By the grouping the Adams locomotives were mostly relegated to secondary duties, their numbers having been depleted further by the loss of 50 0395s requisitioned for the war effort and sent overseas, never to return. Four were lost when the *Arabic* was torpedoed and sunk in the Mediterranean. The bulk of the workhorses were of course Drummond engines, starting with the successful M7 0-4-4 tanks of 1897,105 eventually being built. They were followed by the notorious T7 4-2-2-0, which is reputed to have spent more time being repaired than it did in traffic. The much rated 700 class 0-6-0s (universally known as 'black motors') and a long line of successful 4-4-0s which included the T9s, then followed. Drummond's next designs were the less successful 4-6-0s, of classes F13/E14/G14/P14, all eventually ending up being (nominally) rebuilt or discarded. The T14s however, fared better through being superheated by Urie and later fully modernised by Maunsell in the early 30s, all but one surviving to be taken over by BR. The last Drummond design was for an inside-cylindered 4-4-0 of class D15: the ten engines of this class were said to be the best steamers and fastest runners of all the Drummond classes.

Robert Urie became Chief Mechanical Engineer following Drummond's unfortunate death in 1912; his main contribution was the first successful 4-6-0 designs for the L&SWR. The first ten H15s, appeared in 1913/4, the rebuilding of the E14 335 as an H15 adding an extra one. These 11 engines were well and truly tested over the next few years being put to work on many of the heavy troop and material trains to and from Southampton docks, for the war effort. Towards the end of the war the first ten of the twenty N15 passenger 4-6-0s started to enter service, 17 being in traffic before the grouping. The first 10 N15s were quickly

L&SWR	Passenger Tender Engines	446
	Goods Tender Engines	96
	Passenger Tank Engines	283
	Goods Tank Engines	5
	Shunting Tank Engines	87
	Sub Total	*917*
LB&SCR	Passenger Tender Engines	95
	Goods Tender Engines	83
	Passenger Tank Engines	264
	Goods Tank Engines	167
	Shunting Tank Engines	10
	Sub Total	*619*
SE&CR	Passenger Tender Engines	248
	Goods Tender Engines	216
	Passenger Tank Engines	228
	Goods Tank Engines	34
	Shunting Tank Engines	3
	Sub Total	*729*
IOW	Passenger Tank Engines	18
PD&SWJR	Passenger Tank Engines	2
	Shunting Tank Engine	1
	Total of absorbed locomotives	*2286*

Two LB&SCR Crystal Palace electrification 3-car loose-coupled sets approaching Pouparts Junction (between Clapham Junction and Battersea Park) on the Up Slow Line. In the background can be seen the L&SWR centre carriage sidings which are mainly through sidings that can be accessed from West London Junction and Clapham Junction A signal boxes and lead directly into the main carriage sidings between the LSW mainline and the Windsor lines, known as Clapham Yard. There is an interesting collection of stock in the sidings including a 4-set of corridors with a Restaurant Car marshalled next to the brake end in the formation. The LSW overhead signal gantry spans all the tracks and carries signals for both up and down lines.

followed by the 20 S15 goods version in 1920/21 and the tank versions: four G16 4-8-0T engines for shunting the hump at Feltham and five H16 4-6-2 tanks for cross-London goods transfer traffic, all appearing in 1921/2.

Before taking a look at the detail of the contribution the Brighton made to the locomotive stock of the new company, a word or two about the differences that set them apart from the locos of the L&SWR and the SE&CR would not go amiss. In the first instance all the Brighton engines were equipped with the Westinghouse air brake, as of course was the stock; at the grouping relatively few were dual fitted for working trains to and from other lines. This feature limited their usefulness when working off the Brighton network as few other lines used the air brake, only the Great Eastern having any quantity of air-braked stock. The other point to remember is that as over 70% of the fleet were tank engines this also had the effect of limiting the distances they could run without having to stop for water, further reducing their flexibility when required to work off their native section. The larger engines, in their original form, were also foul of the new SR composite loading gauge: most commonly it was the commodious cab that had to be modified before they could work off the Brighton section without restriction.

The Brighton locomotives that passed to Southern in 1923 ranged from the remaining 11 LB&SCR owned survivors of the A1 & A1X classes to the massive (by comparison) J1/J2 4-6-2 tanks and of course the much loved H1/H2 4-4-2 atlantics. Mention the Brighton almost anywhere and it's the 'Terrier' that will most likely spring to mind. Most of the Southern's constituents had at least one on their books, due to the Brighton having sold many of them out of service to other operators. As a result the Southern also inherited: one each from the L&SWR and SE&CR, one from the FYNR and four from the IWCR. The newly formed Southern Railway inherited a further 219 engines designed by Stroudley who was the LB&SCR's Locomotive Superintendent from 1870 – 1889. During his reign Stroudley had made a considerable attempt at standardisation within the loco department at Brighton. He was followed by R J Billinton who, apart from introducing his own designs, made some alterations to his predecessor's last design, the F class 0-6-2T (one example) later to become the E3 class (16 examples). His first locomotive design, the D3 0-4-4T, eventually numbering 36 engines, first appeared in 1892. The C2 0-6-0s were not far behind, the first of the 55 engines arriving in 1893 from the Vulcan Foundry, which gave rise to their nickname of 'Vulcans'. There then followed 24 B2 4-4-0s and the one B3 before the next tranche of 74 0-6-2 radial tanks of the E4 class: these locos became particularly well known as they were to be found at work on all three divisions of the Southern at one time or another. In 1899 the first of a total of 33 B4 4-4-0s emerged from Brighton Works, followed by two more in 1900, a further 25

coming from Sharp Stewart and five from Brighton Works in 1901/2. These locomotives were intended to be an enlarged and more powerful version of the less than effective B2's and they certainly lasted longer, including the 12 that were nominally rebuilt with even larger boilers by his son! The 30 E5 and 12 E6 0-6-2 radial tanks were to be the last of R J Billinton's designs: the last two engines of the E6 class were originally intended to be 0-8-0 tanks but the order was changed to 0-6-2s by his successor.

It was D Earle Marsh that took over the reins for the next seven years, his first design being for the H1 Atlantics, which also heralded the start of a new era for Brighton locomotive design. These five locomotives were far bigger and more powerful than anything that had gone before. They were built by Kitson's in Leeds, the first one No. 37 in 1905. The other four followed in 1906 and as with the later H2s they very much followed the design principles of Ivatt's GNR Atlantics, which is hardly surprising as Marsh worked at Doncaster under Ivatt prior to his appointment as Locomotive Superintendent for the LB&SCR. Marsh's other classes were the 10 C3 0-6-0 'Horsham' goods engines, the various I classes (1-4) totalling 62 engines and the two J class (officially J1 & J2) 4-6-2 tanks Nos. 325 and 326. Marsh was also the architect of a re-boilering programme, to upgrade many classes of Brighton engines, which at the time had a bit of a reputation for being shy of steam, thus effectively giving them a new lease of life.

The last Locomotive Superintendent of the LB&SCR was L B Billinton, son of the late R J Billinton. He had been with the LB&SCR since leaving school and officially took over on 1st January 1912, after deputising for Marsh during his absence, following illness. In some respects things continued along much the same lines with the building of the last of the H2s and the completion of J class tank No. 326, together with the steady programme of re-boilerings and rebuildings started by his predecessor. L B Billinton's first design was for the E2 0-6-0 shunting tanks, the first five of which appeared in mid-1913, and a further batch of five with larger side tanks was built in 1915/16. His next design, which chronologically speaking came out a few months after the first E2s in Sept. 1913 was for the K class 2-6-0, with four of the first five of these very useful engines being in traffic before the start of the war: another batch of five was added in 1916 and the last seven were built in 1920/21, bringing the class total to 17 in all. His last design, a fitting "swan song", was the impressive L class 4-6-4 Baltic tanks, all seven engines of the class subsequently being rebuilt by Maunsell as tender locos.

We now come to the locomotive inheritance from the SE&CR, where the circumstances were very different to those on either the L&SWR or the LB&SCR. Even after the expenditure of many millions on upgrading, the line was still incapable of taking anything much bigger than a

The original junction for the Southampton and Salisbury lines was a flat junction at Battledown, an early signal box being provided by 1869. The present day Battledown Flyover and a realigned junction came into use in 1897. New signal boxes were provided at Battledown and Worting in connection the work. Records suggest that a further new signal box was provided in December 1904, reputedly a few yards nearer to Worting but as they were both type 4A's and the lever nos. were mostly the same it is possible that it was the 1897 box moved and the not very old frame (5 years) relocked. Battledown lost its signal box altogether in 1925 when all the points and signals were removed and the junction effectively became Worting.

moderate sized 4-4-0, the L class not being built until the axle-weight limit was raised from 18 tons to 19 ¼ tons on most of the old LCDR main line in 1914. Consequently the Southern inherited a fleet of inside cylindered 4-4-0s and 0-6-0s that would have done Derby proud, many of the Maunsell rebuilds even looking the part with their Derby-style cabs and Belpaire boilers. The result was a railway where small locomotives were the order of the day and double-heading was commonplace. It was also a very expensive railway to operate. By the time of the grouping in 1923 many of the old engines that passed to the SE&CR managing committee in 1899 from the LCDR and the SER were either gone, rebuilt or surviving on the steam-worked suburban services of the SE&CR but most didn't last long under their new owners; however, there were exceptions.

As mentioned earlier the development of proposals to electrify the SE&CR's lines around London was thwarted by the continuing expense of the upgrading works and the outbreak of the First World War in 1914. The knock-on effect on the locomotive fleet was that many locos that would have been candidates for the scrap line, in the event of electrification, had to be overhauled and run on, in many cases for a further 10 years or more. The 36 Kirtley-designed A, A1 & A2 0-4-4T engines for the LC&DR fell into this category as did the 32 survivors of the 118 Stirling Q class 0-4-4 tanks built for the SER between 1881 and 1897. H S Wainwright, the SE&CR's Locomotive Superintendent from 1899 – 1913, ended up rebuilding 55 of them with H class boilers, becoming class Q1: even then only 47 survived long enough to become SR

stock. Other Kirtley designs that survived into Southern days were: two of the B1 and all six of the B2 0-6-0 goods engines, most of them surviving for a further 10 years. The 10 T class 0-6-0 tanks mostly had long and useful lives but by 1923 the survivors of the M series of 4-4-0s were getting thin on the ground, with all the original Ms gone and just one each of the M1 & M2s left. By this time it was only the class of 26 M3s dating from 1891 that were left intact but they didn't last long, the whole class disappearing by the end of 1928.

Returning now to the rest of the locomotives bequeathed by James Stirling, Locomotive Superintendent of the SER from 1878 – 1898, and that subsequently ended up with the Southern Railway, after 1923, the oldest of these were the O class 0-6-0's that were built over a 21-year period between 1878 and 1899. Once again Wainwright rebuilt many of them, 58 in all, with the ubiquitous H class boiler, a new C class style cab (in most cases) and other modifications. Consequently all except No. 282 survived to be taken over by the Southern and 29 of the original engines were also taken into Southern stock, four engines being sold on to the Light Railways in Kent over the years. The 88 F class 4-4-0s dating from 1883 to 1898 were soon outclassed as train weights increased: 76 of them were given the Wainwright treatment from 1903 onwards, with new cabs and boilers. It must have worked as a few were still at work over 40 years after rebuilding. Stirling's other 4-4-0 design, the B class of 1898, also received similar treatment, turning them into B1s, 27 out of the 29 locos eventually being upgraded this way with just

Clapham Junction North signal box. This view was probably taken on 22 May 1911 judging by the two policemen and three guardsmen on duty. This was also the time of the railway strike of that year, the presence of the military possibly more of a deterrent to sabotage. This was also the day that King George V opened the "Festival of Empire" at the Crystal Palace as well as being the official opening day for the new electric services between Victoria and Crystal Palace. The new electric services between London Bridge and Crystal Palace had to wait more than a further year because the contracted power company were unable to provide the necessary supplies.

over half passing into BR ownership at nationalisation. The last design of James Stirling that we will look at is the R and R1 0-6-0 tanks. There were originally 25 R class locos ordered in 1888 but it took Ashford ten years to build them and 24 of the 25 locomotives were handed over to the Southern at the grouping, the 13 rebuilds having been given H class boilers with most receiving Wainwright cabs as well, turning them in to R1s.

We now come to the designs of H S Wainwright or perhaps more correctly those of Robert Surtees, because on locomotive matters he was the man behind the throne. Wainwright was really a Carriage and Wagon man, with a good working knowledge of locomotive design. Following his appointment, his first task was to develop plans to upgrade the locomotive stock of the new SE&CR, in order that the locomotive fleet would be capable of working the heavier trains that would be running once the various sections of line had been improved. In the interim however, existing axle-loads and restrictions had to be observed. Under Wainwright's guidance a two-pronged approach was developed, which amounted to a strategy of

build new and upgrade the best of the existing fleet. The various improvements carried out to some classes of inherited locomotives have already been covered. It only needs noting that the process generally took the form of reboilering and the provision of a Wainwright style cab, with a few locos receiving new cylinders as well. The build new part of the strategy involved the provision of significant numbers of standard 'go anywhere' locomotives from a standardised range of parts to reduce costs and spares holdings.

The first class of locomotives introduced under Wainwright's stewardship numbered just five locomotives: they were part of an 1899 order for ten 4-4-0 locomotives being built for the Great North of Scotland Railway by Neilson Reid & Co. The GNofSR cancelled five of the class and somehow they were offered to the SE&CR, whether by direct approach to Wainwright or to a board member is probably now lost in history. At that time they were useful enough but because they were non-standard they were likely to be destined to have short lives and so it was; they became the G class. all five of them surviving to become Southern property (just) but they were all gone within four years. In 1900 the first 34 of an eventual 109 C class 0-6-0s started to arrive from: Ashford 14, Neilson Reid 15 and Sharp Stewart five; the next 20 arrived in 1901. The fact that 53 of them were still in service at the start of 1962, over 60 years later, says it all. The remaining members of the class were withdrawn by the end of the year. Another Wainwright – Surtees masterpiece took to the rails in 1901 with the first 11 of the D class 4-4-0s joining the ranks of new engines being delivered to SE&CR, another 40 being built over the next five years. By any standards the rate of renewal of the locomotive fleet represented a massive investment but it didn't stop there, as new locomotives kept arriving throughout the early years of the century. 1904 saw the introduction of the H class 0-4-4 tanks, seven being built at Ashford. They were followed by a further 57 engines over the next six years, and two more were erected in 1915, when Maunsell conducted an audit at Ashford and discovered that only 64 Hs had been built, out of the 66 ordered. By 1905 attention had been turned to the introduction of the E class 4-4-0s. These 26 locomotives were built with Belpaire fireboxes from the start and some were given extended smoke boxes as early as 1908, even before the last few entered traffic in 1909/10. There was a gap of four years before the first of the diminutive P class 0-6-0 tanks appeared in 1909: this class of only eight engines were intended for the light-weight push and pull services of the time. Unfortunately they were really too late on the scene and somewhat underpowered, particularly for the revised services and heaver stock used after the war. Amazingly they found a new role as shunting tanks on the lightly-laid lines of the many docks and depots that are found around the south coast. The last truly Wainwright –Surtees design was for the J class 0-6-4 tanks, originally intended for the Tonbridge and Hastings business services. They spent most of their lives working the London - Redhill services, following the introduction of the L class engines.

The L class 4-4-0's were the final class accredited to Wainwright but in fact they were not ordered until after his retirement. The drawings produced by Surtees a year earlier, were dusted off in anticipation of the increase in maximum axle weights permitted on the Chatham main line to 19¼ tons in 1914 and presented to Maunsell for his authorisation upon arrival. As with any new chief anxious to make his mark, this was not forthcoming until certain modifications had been incorporated, particularly to the cab, smokebox layout, chimney and valves, following consultations with his former Chief Draughtsman at Inchicore. R E L Maunsell was the SE&CR's first and last Chief Mechanical Engineer; Wainwright, was of course, their only Locomotive Superintendent. The main part of Maunsell's contribution to the Southern Railway's locomotive history really belongs to the years following the grouping. However, his first two or three designs (depending on which way you look at it) belong to the

SE&CR era and the first of them began life just before the First World War. Soon after arriving at Ashford, Maunsell produced his first design for the N class 2-6-0, which was worked up during 1914. The first locomotive being completed in July 1917, five more followed in 1920 and six in 1922. They were like nothing seen at Ashford before, with a Swindon-style taper boiler, outside cylinders with Walschaert's valve gear, not to mention the Midland style cab. It was this design that the government decided to perpetuate after the war, as it was very close to the proposed Association of Railway Locomotive Engineers (ARLE) 2-6-0 which was based on the N class design: but at the time the ARLE 2-6-0 design was incomplete. Subsequently 100 sets of parts, together with boilers, were ordered, from Woolwich Arsenal in 1919, to provide employment. Following difficulties the boilers were eventually supplied by outside contractors. Maunsell's second design, using the same boiler, was for a 2-6-4 tank engine version, known as the K class. Only one engine was completed during the SE&CR's separate existence, No. 790 in June 1917 (just before the first N class). Under the Southern a further 20 engines were ordered and they subsequently became better known as the River class, being named after rivers in the Southern territory, No. 790 was named River Avon in 1925. The last Maunsell design to be built (well, partly) before the grouping, was the N1 three-cylinder version of the N class. The first member of what became a very small sub class, No. 822, was outshopped from Ashford in March 1923 and therefore is strictly a Southern engine. I will pick up the story again later in the series, after the grouping, as these locomotives are very much a part of Southern Railway's history.

As can be seen all the locomotive engineers from the constituent companies that formed the Southern group were adept at rebuilding locomotives, principally to extend their working lives and improve performance. The first Maunsell rebuild of C class No. 685 as a saddle tank in 1917, was for the purely practical purpose, of providing a cost-effective locomotive, for shunting at Bricklayers Arms goods depot. By the early years of the 20th century many locomotives designed in the 1880s and 90s were outclassed by new designs with larger boilers. As, to coin a phrase, "they were only half worn out", many were given a new boiler, often with the addition of a superheater, which then resulted in an extended smokebox being required. In turn this led to the appearance of the locomotive being changed markedly. Maunsell took this a stage further when he rebuilt E class 4-4-0 No. 179 in 1919, to haul the anticipated 300 ton continental expresses out of Victoria via the Chatham route, which was still restricted at this time and the L class were still barred. The locomotive was transformed, both in appearance and performance. The modifications consisted of: new cylinders, ten-inch piston valves, an enlarged Belpaire firebox, superheater, top feed, Midland style cab: and it still weighed in at over a ton less than an original E class. A further ten engines were sent to

Beyer Peacock & Co to be rebuilt in 1920, some lasting for another 40 years. Following this success Maunsell sent ten D class 4-4-0's to Beyer Peacock for similar treatment in 1921, and again the resulting rebuild was an outstanding success. Two more Ds were modified at Ashford in 1922 and a further nine in 1926/7. While Maunsell was Works Manager at Inchicore he designed and built a single 4-4-0 locomotive No. 341 for the Great Southern & Western Railway in 1913, and the family likeness to the E1 and D1 rebuilds; and the later L1s is quite striking. (A drawing and details of this locomotive appear in *'Maunsell Locomotives a Pictorial History', pages 18 & 19.*)

There were also a few locomotives inherited by the Southern Railway from its main constituents that are not covered above and that should be mentioned. All of these locomotives originally started life as fairly standard contractor's models. There was a Manning, Wardle contractors' 0-6-0 saddle tank that shunted Ashford Works and an even older Manning, Wardle 0-6-0 dating from 1879 that pottered around Folkestone Harbour and was sold out of service by the Southern in 1925. There was yet another Manning, Wardle locomotive, this time a 0-4-0ST that was originally purchased by James Stirling back in 1881 for working at Folkestone. This one was given an overhaul in 1925 and then given the number 225S in the departmental series, before being dispatched to Meldon Quarry as the shunter, where it lasted until 1938. The South Eastern also had two crane tanks of Neilson origin that worked at various places from time to time; though one was normally to be found at Ashford Works. These two also had various numbers in capital stock and on the service list, during their life-times.

The South Western's contribution to the miscellany was the last four remaining dock tanks from the Southampton Dock Company, which became part of the L&SWR in 1892 (see part 1). They were 0-4-0STs in two classes, the two members of the 0111 class built by the Vulcan Foundry in 1878 were No. 118 *Vulcan* (latter renumbered 111) and No. 408 *Bretwalda*. Both were withdrawn during 1924, *Bretwalda* being sold on. The other two engines belonged to the 0458 class, built by Hawthorn Leslie, in 1890: they were No. 457 *Clausentum* and No. 458 *Ironside*. Both survived far longer than the Vulcans, No. 458 *Ironside* surviving long enough as the shed pilot at Guildford to receive its BR No. 30458.

Another contribution to this diverse locomotive heritage came from the PD&SWJR in the form of three more of Hawthorn Leslie's products; these were much bigger locomotives than the Dock Tanks, all dating from 1907 when the East Cornwall Minerals Railway was regauged from 3ft 6in to standard gauge. One 0-6-0T *A S Harris* and two 0-6-2T *Lord St Levan* and *Earl of Mount Edgcumbe* respectively, they were numbered 756, 757 and 758 by the Southern and all three survived long enough to become BR stock.

By the time of the amalgamation the locomotive stud on the Isle of Wight had been rationalised somewhat but there were still 18 locomotives to be taken into SR stock. The list consisted of five Brighton "Terriers" (as noted in the LB&SCR notes), a Manning, Wardle contractors' 0-6-0ST very similar to the others of this type inherited by the Southern but of a very much later date: only being built in 1902, it was the newest locomotive on the island. The other oddity was a 4-4-0T of 1890 vintage built by Black, Hawthorn and supplied new to the IWCR. The remaining eleven locomotives were all 2-4-0 tanks, of similar design, manufactured by Beyer Peacock between 1864 and 1898. With one exception they were all supplied new, three to the IWCR and seven to the IWR. The exception was a second hand example originally supplied to the Swindon & Marlborough Railway (later M&SWJR) where it was their No. 6. It was sold to the IWCR in 1906, becoming No. 7 in the IWCR list.

Following on from the detailed review of the motive power fleet, inherited by the new Southern Railway, it is time to take a look at the rolling stock that was handed on to the new organisation. As you would expect the Southern inherited, at 7,500 vehicles, proportionally more passenger carriages than any of the other three big four railways, for example, the Great Western with over 3,000 route miles as against the Southern's 2,178 route miles, had over 1,000 less passenger carriages. The LMS and the LNER each had considerably more but then the route mileages in both these cases were more than treble that of the Southern. However, the inheritance in this case could, in some ways, be described as a bit of a liability. Only the L&SWR had any quantity of corridor carriages and only a few could be described as modern. The LB&SCR on the other hand had very few corridor vehicles and they were generally to be found running in the formation of the mainly first class business expresses along with a couple of Pullman cars to provide the 'high end' catering facilities. The situation on the SE&CR, with regard to corridor stock was little better. Even with the arrival of Maunsell (9 years before) there were still only 15 Brake Composites (of Wainwright origin), six Corridor Thirds, the first eight car set of continentals and the 15 American-style vestibule cars inherited from the SER in traffic by 1923. It follows then that the vast majority of carriages inherited by the Southern were of the compartment type, with a fair smattering of them with access to a lavatory from at least a couple of compartments or a saloon.

The South Western alone had managed to build corridor stock in any quantity. Even then the early turn-of-the-century panelled vehicles were formed into sets, with the gangway connection only within the set, the brake vehicles only having a connection at the compartment end. By 1923 the first of the Ironclad stock was also entering service but with just two sets for boat train traffic and four sets working on the Bournemouth line they were still spread thinly on the ground. A further six sets were on order for Portsmouth and Bournemouth services. When it came to the provision of electric trains for the L&SWR

Waterloo Station on what looks like a cold March 21 1922 on the occasion of the formal opening of the rebuilt station and dedication of the Victory Arch, by Queen Mary who was deputising for the King who had a bad cold. On the left hand column of the Arch the names of the 585 L&SWR staff that died during the First World War were inscribed.

electrification scheme, a decision was taken to make use of some of the comparatively new bogie block sets that would otherwise be redundant if new stock were provided. Hence 63 four-car bogie block sets dating from the early years of the century were converted (recycled!) into 84 three-car electric sets, the first sets being completed towards the end of 1914. Later, after the war in 1919, authority was given to provide 24 unpowered two-car trailer sets, from 12 bogie block sets, for use during the peak services and at other busy times. These trailer sets were marshalled between two three-car units. While on the subject of the steam-hauled bogie block sets, many of the remaining sets were spilt to form two-car branch line sets, at least ten of which became push-pull sets. The remaining non-corridor stock passed to the new company and as many of the vehicles were comparatively new they lasted a good many years. Most of the older stock and the few remaining L&SW four- and six-wheelers did not last long after the grouping but there were some interesting exceptions.

On the LB&SCR, apart from the few 'Balloon' corridor vehicles, just about all the other carriage stock was of the compartment type. A few vehicles had side corridors but without the internal compartment partitions along the corridor: they were formed in pairs as push-pull sets with a gangway between the two vehicles. Initially they were used on services between Brighton and Worthing or on the Littlehampton, Arundel, Ford and Bognor local services, being very convenient for fare collection. The few corridor coaches and the vast majority of compartment coaches were of the bogie type but the Brighton were still using some four-wheel carriages. Many dated from the 1870s and had been built to work as block sets with Stroudley's 0-6-0 'Terrier's on the London area suburban network: needless to say these old vehicles were amongst the first for the chop but a few survived and lived to fight another day as we shall see later in the series.

For the South London electrification new stock was ordered. Eight three-car trains were ordered from the Metropolitan Amalgamated Carriage & Wagon Co., Ltd of Birmingham: there were 16 third class motor coaches and eight first class trailers formed as: motor third, trailer first, motor third. At 63ft. 7in. long and 9ft. 3in. wide they were longer and wider than other LB & SCR stock, but it was soon found that too much first class accommodation had been provided, and between 1910 and 1912 the sets were spilt up and 16 two-car sets were formed by coupling a

Above - D1 4-4-0 No. 494 built by Dubs & Co as a D class in 1903, Maunsell had it rebuilt into a D1 Class by Beyer Peacock's in 1921. The rebuilds had particularly long lives, this one surviving until August 1960. In this shot the engine is probably not long back from being rebuilt as is still painted in the SE&CR wartime livery of all over dark grey with just the number on the tender. The picture must have been taken in the early 1920's with the engine working what appears to be a train of L&NWR stock.

Bottom - The leading unit is a L&SWR 3 SUB unit converted from bogie block stock, the centre two cars are an unpowered pair of trailers cars, originally 24 of these 2-car sets were provided and others were added at various times. The trailer sets were used for peak hour strengthening, this pair is interesting in that they are formed of LB&SC stock and only a few trailer sets were thus formed. The final 3 SUB unit is also formed from converted LB&SCR stock.

driving trailer, to each motor car. The driving trailers were converted from conventional stock (ex-suburban sets) 57ft. 7in. long 8ft. wide with a motorman's driving cab, two first class and six third class compartments. The spare first class trailers were fitted up for steam working and redeployed on the Brighton main line. When it came to providing electric stock for the Crystal Palace extension the formation of the units was changed to: driving motor third, driving trailer composite, driving trailer composite. All the new vehicles were 57ft. 7in. over the buffers, with 8ft. wide bodies in order to pass through Crystal Palace tunnel, which at the time had restrictions on the length and width of stock the could pass through it. The order for the new stock was split between the Metropolitan Amalgamated Carriage & Wagon Co., Ltd. and the Brighton's own carriage works at Lancing, as follows: 30 driving motor coaches and 30 driving trailer composites from the former and 30 driving trailer composites from the latter. After a couple of years the standard set formation was changed to: driving trailer composite, driving motor coach, driving trailer composite, and it was not unknown for these sets to operate in two-car formation particularly when used for strengthening purposes. It was comparatively easy to alter the makeup of all the Brighton electric sets as they were loose-coupled and not in fixed formations as the L&SWR sets were, and individual vehicles were changed round from time to time.

The SE&CR having not proceeded with electrification was the only one of the three main constituents to pass on a wholly steam-hauled carriage fleet. As mentioned above the South Eastern had very few corridor vehicles (44 by my reckoning), it therefore follows that the vast majority would have been of the compartment type. Those vehicles that were subsequently built by SE&CR were mostly of what has become known as the 'Birdcage stock' type, only the brake versions having the actual 'Birdcage', eliminated on most of the later builds. The real problem was that much of the remaining stock that was inherited from the SER and the LC&DR and then subsequently passed on to the Southern in 1923 was of the four and six wheel varieties. Some of the LC&DR stock that dated from the 1880s and 90s was modified by the SE&CR, during and after the war, by the removal of the centre wheel set and the fitting of truss rods to compensate for the loss of support. They were also fitted with the, South Eastern preferred, vacuum brake, steam heating and electric lighting. Many of them were formed into five-coach sets and were used on London suburban workings; another case of having to keep things going pending electrification. Given the investment in these carriages they were prime candidates for being cascaded on when electrification finally arrived on the South Eastern and Chatham sections: they and their very similar 40ft to 46ft long bogie cousins went on to enjoy particularly long lives and we will come across them again later in the series.

The Southern also inherited passenger stock from the absorbed companies namely the PD&SWJR and the lines on the Isle of Wight. As mentioned in part 1 the PD&SWJR only ran independent services over the Bere Alston to Callington section, of their line, and they did this mostly with second-hand stock acquired from the L&SWR. The early services used mostly ex- L&SWR four-wheelers but they had been replaced in 1921 by four early L&SWR arc-roofed bogie coaches dating from the early 1880s, hence they returned to the L&SWR when it took over in 1922 and were passed on to the Southern. A couple of them were very quickly cascaded on elsewhere.

The Isle of Wight must have seemed like a nightmare when the L&SWR's directors toured the island in late 1921, with just four bogie carriages on the island. Of the four, two were built new for the IWC in 1890 by the Lancaster Carriage and Wagon Company, one was bought second-hand from the Midland Railway and was a originally a brake composite with a clerestory roof and six-wheel bogies but by 1923 the clerestory had gone and the bogies had been replaced with four-wheel replacements, obtained from Derby. The last of the four started life as the carriage end of the IWC's railmotor unit which was converted into a brake third in 1913, using a spare bogie obtained from the LSW, following condemnation of the railmotor's business end. By the grouping most of the remaining four-wheelers were hand-me- downs from such diverse companies as the: Great Eastern Railway, North London Railway, Manchester Sheffield and Lincolnshire Railway and the good old L&SWR. I doubt that they (the directors) looked on these relics from the L&SWR's past as old friends and as you might have guessed only three survived long enough to receive their new Southern numbers. Probably the most interesting carriages that were on the island at the time of the grouping were the eighteen ex-Metropolitan vehicles owned by the IWR. At first glance they looked like bogie coaches but they weren't: the middle wheel sets were rigid like a four-wheeler and the outer wheel sets had extra side play, controlled by a swing link arrangement. Few if any of the island coaches were fitted up for steam heating but at least these had electric light, which many did not.

It now remains to say a few words about the goods stock that the various organisations brought to the party. As recorded by many observers over the years the three constituent companies of the newly formed Southern Railway relied heavily on their passenger traffic to generate the majority of their income. The goods traffic, more commonly referred to as freight on the Southern, represented about a third of the total income for the new group. For the other three companies formed at the grouping, the goods receipts represented more than half their total income. Naturally this situation was reflected in the relatively low numbers of goods wagons owned by the Southern group and was quoted by Dendy Marshall as 36,749. *An Illustrated History of Southern Wagons* (various volumes) by G Bixley, A Blackburn, R Chorley and M King records the figure of 36,096 for mainland based stock, an additional 563 for the Isle of Wight and a probable 45 from the PD&SWJR, giving a total of 36,704 for the 1st January 1923. This leaves a discrepancy of 45 and is yet another instance of the figures from different sources not quite adding up.

Having now set the scene as it was at the Grouping, in the next part of the story we will look at 'The priorities' and the decisions that were forced on the new company by circumstance rather than choice. My thanks go to Martin Stone for independently checking through the manuscript, providing comment and additional input as part of the process.

TO BE CONTINUED

Right - A little after the period of this article but a great example of the output of the Southern's publicity machine that was about to start shaping the image of the new company.

Bottom - The LBSCR's meagre contribution to the Southern's fleet of corridor coaches was confined to a few sets of "Balloon stock" with the addition of the odd Pullman car to provide the catering. These "Balloon" sets were mainly confined to a few mostly first class business trains or, as here, the "Continental Express London & Newhaven" which ran between Victoria and Newhaven.

The photographs accompanying this article are all from the RCHS Spence collection.

MONEY-SAVING PROVERBS *for* 1930

WHAT'S THERE ON THE BILL COMES OUT OF THE BOOKING OFFICE

SR

A DISAPPOINTED MAN

When looking at railway history we make no excuses in often romanticising the past: a perception of life past viewed through rose tinted spectacles. But we should not forget that the Southern Railway, in this no different from any of the other pre-nationalisation concerns, was first and foremost a business. The fact it carried passengers and goods was secondary to the principal aim of the business: making money: money for investors, the shareholders. Naturally it achieved this through its public service business, in so doing providing useful employment and invariably a pension for its employees. In this respect, and for employees of all grades, a job on the railway was sought after and invariably valued: safe and secure, with due acknowledgment to come, or so it was believed, when eventually came the time to retire.

But there was another side to the Southern, hidden away in the accounts department. We must not forget that it was still a company that would not spend or waste money and that included unnecessary spending on staff matters.

Albert Farrent started his railway career on the LBSCR in May 1887. His grandson, Ken Gates, knows little of his ancestor's life, save for the fact that his grandfather was with the locomotive department throughout, initially at Battersea, where this photograph was taken of him on the footplate of No 176, a 'Gladstone' 0-4-2. He does know that at one stage Albert was involved in an accident, presumably at work, the consequence being that a plate was inserted into his skull. Despite this he resumed his footplate career.

Albert would have completed his 50 years on the railway on 5th May 1937. But to achieve this he would have to go into a new pay week, with just one day left to serve. Consequently he was compelled to retire after 49 years 364 days service. Having then failed to achieve the requisite 50 years, he was denied the recognition of that achievement from his employers, a gold watch.

There may of course be more to the story, but this is what Albert handed down. Proof (if needed) came from his trade union, ASLEF, which on learning of the situation, made their own presentation to Albert of a clock. Even so, still a disappointing end to a lifelong career.   With grateful thanks to Ken Gates.

RECOLLECTIONS OF THE
A.C.E.
Maurice Hopper

To catch the weekday 11 o'clock from Waterloo we have to leave Ashtead on the 9.30 am, arriving at Waterloo at 10.3 am, which only stops at Wimbledon after Motspur Park. The 9.50 am, with its arrival at 10.22 am, is considered to be the "back-up" train, while the 09.57 am, arrival at 10.44 am, after a change at Epsom, is seen as "cutting it too fine".[1] This probably over cautious travel planning by my rather anxious mother is based on concerns about missing the ACE. However, the next departure from Waterloo to the west at 1.00 pm will arrive at our destination nearly 3 hours and 20 minutes later than the Atlantic Coast Express.

The extra time at Waterloo is not wasted. There is always plenty to see and do, with the music to listen too, the need to pop into Boots or pick up a newspaper from W. H. Smith's. The expectation of the most important departure of the day builds up. There are comfortable wooden seats for mother to sit on while we wait for the station announcer to tell us under which letter the queue is forming. As regular travellers we know the empty stock, which we have already seen as we came through Clapham Junction, will be pulled into Platform 11 next to the cab road.

Once the queue is moving through the ticket inspection at the barrier, with information being given about which portion of our train we need to be in, there is a steady flow of people down the platform. The North Devon portions of the ACE are always at the front. Mixed in with the people are trolleys of luggage, stores for the buffet and the restaurant car and more platform staff to help people find their seats.

Our reserved seats are labelled with fawn coloured cards, with red printing and hand-written numbers and destinations. We find our seats are in the Ilfracombe portion of the train which is formed of early Bulleid stock with 'suburban' style compartment doors.

We switch to the Torrington portion, which has the more attractive big picture windows. Once we have 'reserved' our, now unlabelled, seats with the paper and coats, mother will go to the restaurant car to get tickets for the first sitting for lunch, while I will go to the front of the train to see the engine backing down and coupling up.

While walking down the platform, we have seen the 'Tavern Car', in this case the White Horse, Bulleid's 'local' in Dorking. Its brick and half timbered livery has given way to an inn sign painted on a large area of green below the shallow top windows of the bar area. We will later walk through the timbered and 'plastered' bar on our return from lunch, but I am getting ahead of myself.

With a great deal of whistling along the platform, and between the engines, our train moves forward over the crossings to join the down mainline. Even towards the front of the train, one can feel the push from the loco at the back. This is especially so if our 'Merchant Navy' starts to slip.

After Vauxhall, our train gathers speed only to slow for the curve at Clapham Junction. Speeding on, I always watched out for the Wimbledon flyover, as we usually only go over this on local services rather than having the excitement of going under it, with clouds of smoke and steam hanging under the concrete. After Raynes Park, and the divergence of our more regular line to Epsom, there are less familiar things to see. This observation from the train is assisted by a copy of Alan Anderson's 'Devon Belle', subtitled Famous Train Journeys No. 2. (I think No. 1 was the Flying Scotsman.) the end paper maps and the gradient diagrams at the back are most important information in this little volume. I can quietly monitor the progress of our train, which is a great joy to my mother, who is able to settle down, undisturbed, with her Manchester Guardian.[2]

Undisturbed that is until the ticket collector

Opposite top - On a summer Saturday, the cab-road between platforms 11 and 12 has been given over to queues of passengers. With the clock at 10.6, many will be waiting for the multi-train A.C.E, rather than the multi-portioned train described in this article. While not so common on a weekday, such scenes rank alongside pre-motorway holiday traffic queues and crowded airport departure lounges in the history of British holiday travel since 1945.

Opposite bottom - Templecombe, like so many of the stations between Salisbury and Exeter, was not well served by the A.C.E., however the speeding express offered an exciting prospect to the railway photographer. I wonder if they travelled there by train?

The roof of County Hall stands over a 3SUB made into a 4SUB by the addition of a 'fat' Bullied coach and the signal box stands over the Ilfracombe portion of the ACE., while 35016 'Elders Fyffes', showing signs of a recent change in ownership, moves slowly forward under a plume of smoke on its way to the West.

comes through the train. His work is not only to see tickets, but also to double-check that everybody was in the right portion of our train. Having moved with our Ilfracombe tickets into the Torrington portion, we are told this is the wrong part of the train. Our argument about the quality of the windows seems to be of little interest. However, the problem is resolved when the inspector is told we intended to leave the train at Barnstaple Junction. He says he is particularly concerned, as he does not want a complaint from people travelling on first class passes being allowed to travel to the wrong destination. It is our habit to have our passes made out for the furthest destination, although we never seem to use them to go to Ilfracombe for the day.[3]

The attention to passengers being in the correct part of our train through an abundance of staff, coaching stock boards and paper labels is clearly considered a good investment as it saves trouble later by avoiding having to move passengers during shunting operations as the train was divided.

There is another disturbance at Salisbury. While the three-minute stop is used by the engine crew, and a team from the shed, to get the bag in the tender and trim the coal, we would use the time to run back down the platform to join the restaurant car. This saves walking back through, what is often, a very crowded train. As we depart the chorus of sounds to accompany the next stage of our journey starts, the gentle rattle of cutlery, crockery and glasses. The menu on offer is limited and predictable, but does run to three courses. The soup to start is served from a tureen balanced on a towelled arm, followed by chicken or fish served with boiled potatoes and vegetables with a desert of Peach Melba. The final part of the performance is the serving of coffee from simultaneously poured silver jugs of coffee and milk. Service is only interrupted by the crew's knowledge of the track, which must have avoided a fair number of spillages.

Amazingly, the meal is priced at 10/6 (52.5p) and 6/6 (32.5p) for children. This makes the cost of our journey, including the 6d each for the reserved seats, less than fifteen percent of the cost of the fare to the furthest destination, Padstow, which costs about £7.00[4]. My great-aunt in North Devon will no doubt tell us this meal is a great extravagance, so we have learnt not to talk about it during the following week.

On one occasion, the ACE came to a prolonged stop waiting to go through the temporary single line set up during the repair of Buckhorn Weston Tunnel. It was a hot day and the open windows allowed conversations between the men working beside the line and the dining car crew, requests being made for any spare food. There was a very definite sense of the railway's social hierarchy in these exchanges.

On another occasion, the gentleman at the next table spoke with a unique Hampshire burr. It was John Arlott, on his way to that West Country institution, the live, Friday Night, broadcasting of Any Questions. (We listened that evening with rather more than usual interest to his words of wisdom coming from some remote West Country village hall, the Bush portable radio's reproduction interspersed with the crackles of long wave and the call sign of East Germany Radio taken from Beethoven's Ninth, but I must not digress into another story.)

By the time our train is passing Yeovil Junction we are on our way back to our seats, finding our way through the 'Tavern' bar with its internal timber work, little tables with chrome rails around them and generally rather dark atmosphere. The red-tiled floor always seems sticky from the spillage of drinks.

The final stages of this part of our journey are marked by the climbing of Honiton Bank, dashing pass the traffic standing on the A30 at the end of the dual-carriage-way to the west of Honiton, before sitting on the level crossing at Sidmouth Junction, while the through coaches to the East Devon coast are detached. As we approach Exeter, the loco yards at Exmouth Junction stand north of the line before our train enters Mount Pleasant tunnel and finally comes to a stand at the Central Station.

Exeter Central marks a change in mood for the ACE. Like some great symphony, we have pounded our way through two fast movements complete with the coda after the pause at Sidmouth Junction. However, the themes in these movements have been set by what is still to come in the slow movements, the formation of our train being controlled by its division at Exeter.

To some extent, the name of our train is only fifty percent correct. Out of the twelve coaches leaving Waterloo, only six arrived at the Atlantic coast. One is dropped at Salisbury to be attached to the following stopping train to Exeter. Two are dropped at Sidmouth Junction before heading for English Channel resorts, one each for Sidmouth and Exmouth. The main portions from Exeter are for North Devon, being the front three coaches for Ilfracombe and one for Torrington. The second portion is made up of the coaches for Padstow, Bude and Plymouth. Two more coaches for Padstow are added here, while the one-coach portions have extra coaches added at the next division points: Barnstaple Junction, Okehampton

or Halwill Junction. With so many single coach portions, the train has a preponderance of brake composites.

The engines waiting to conduct our divided train forward are 'off stage' through the Queen Street bridge ahead of the arriving train. On arrival the 'Merchant Navy' would be detached and run forward under the over-bridge into the down carriage sidings.

The first away, from the front of the original formation, is the North Devon portion behind a Light Pacific. A few puffs will take our new engine on to the steep bank down to St Davids. The down starter can only be pulled off when the road is set into platform 4 at St Davids, due to the bank that extends right down to the junction with the GWR mainline. As we slip down the bank, it is possible to see the 'Merchant Navy' that has brought us from Waterloo[5] and another Light Pacific ready to back down onto the Plymouth portion. There may also be a banker or two making their way down hill on the front of the Plymouth portion, as there is now plenty of room at the front of the platform to fit them in.[6] Being the ACE, the North Devon portion leaves first, whereas most trains carry the Plymouth portion at the front.

The change of our locomotive and the division of our train take just four minutes for the North Devon departure, but the Plymouth portion will have to wait another thirteen minutes. The station pilot will already be working on the back of the train to remove the restaurant car so it can be serviced and prepared for its return to Waterloo, most likely on the 4.30pm. While all this is happening on the down side of Central Station, on the up side Plymouth and North Devon trains are arriving and being formed into the 2.30 departure for Waterloo.

That we are now in the "slow movement" of this symphony is supported by the evidence from the timetable. After improvements to the timetable in the summer of 1952, the ACE is booked to cover the 83.7 miles from Waterloo to Salisbury in just 83 minutes, the Southern Region's first mile-a-minute timing. The allowance for the 75.9 miles of switchback to Sidmouth Junction was 80 minutes, with 14 minutes being allowed for the final 12 miles to Exeter. East and west of Salisbury, the line makes very different work for the crew, especially the fireman, with prolonged firing on the gentle climb out of the London Basin, and the greater assistance from gravity to rush the banks west of Salisbury.

After Exeter, the portions of the Atlantic Coast Express still had a considerable way to go. The next 55 miles on the North Devon line to Ilfracombe would take the ACE 105 minutes and the 88 miles to Padstow some 165 minutes, rolling in at exactly five o'clock. This is six hours from Waterloo, the first three hours to Exeter being accomplished at around sixty miles an hour and the second half at nearer thirty. For those travelling to the Atlantic Coast this is definitely a journey of two halves.

Our train drops down to Exeter St Davids, providing a sweeping view over the Exe flood plain to the south. At St Davids, we may see a train travelling in the same direction that is going to London Paddington or one travelling in the opposite direction that is going west. This rather confusing situation, for those not familiar with the railway map, is formalised at Cowley Bridge Junction, where our train heads west (which is actually north at this point) taking the 'down branch' (SR) off the 'up main' (GW).

As we travel further along the North Devon Line, the wide valley gives way to a sinuous, narrower and more steep-sided valley, causing the railway to curve from side to side with many crossings of the river. We drift round long curves with the front of our short train visible as the 'West Country' clanks along. The line is punctuated by over-bridges with a separate arch for each track and beyond Copplestone, with passing stations on the single line. Slowing for each of these, we can easily read the names of King's Nympton or Portsmouth Arms as the single-line tablets are exchanged. This adds to the relatively slow progress along the formation built for two tracks as shown by the empty half of the river bridges.

As we arrive at Barnstaple, we can see to the north of our train the Great Western line coming in across the River Taw from Barnstaple Victoria. This is not the lowest railway bridge on the Taw, as the ACE will find its way over the curved bridge to Barnstaple Town on the final leg of its journey to Ilfracombe.

At Barnstaple we leave the train and make our way over the footbridge to the up platform, not to go out of the station like the others leaving the ACE here, but to wait for the up stopping train at 3.45 pm. This will take us back to Chapelton, through which our train rushed about 50 minutes before. Chapelton is closer to my Great Uncle Miles' farm near Yarnscombe. He is standing on the platform as we arrive, talking to Mr. Osman the stationmaster, having completed the purchase of one of Mr Osman's jars of honey. While my Uncle did not use the train very much, perhaps once a year to go "up" to the Royal (Horticultural) Show in London, he got to know Mr Osman well on his arrival in Devon as the farm was moved from Essex by rail in 1951.

Services like the Atlantic Coast Express very quickly became seen as an extravagance for a modern railway. With its demand for the attention of many staff, especially at its division points and the relatively poor use of rolling stock, it was a costly and rather low capacity train. The restaurant facilities were especially vulnerable. With white tablecloths, smart uniforms, silver cutlery and heavy-duty crockery it was easy to see how it would fall foul of the economy drives in the nineteen-sixties. I last met one of the restaurant car conductors single-handedly working the buffet car of a 4BEP unit on a busy Victoria-Dover boat-train in the mid-sixties. I spent sometime doing the washing up for him to help clear the decks.

Postscript

After the line west of Okehampton closed,

Jennings, the Bude coach operator, provided a railway replacement service from the North Coast of Cornwall. Towards the end of the 1990s, this was taken over by the First Group, with coaches carrying the name 'Atlantic Coast Express' and number X9, the afternoon departure of this service from Okehampton being the school bus to Holsworthy. As a former Okehampton College teacher, I was able to carry on something of the 'Southern Way' about this departure by blowing my whistle and giving the driver the "right away", whilst carrying out bus duty at the end of the school day.

However, I suspect few, if any, of the children (or even the bus driver) realised the significance of my attention to this departure. The railway had come to West Devon and had made little impact on the lives of many of the people living there. With its slow decline and almost unnoticed going, rural life carried on regardless. The railway had been gone for twenty-five years, and the train for thirty-five years by the time the name was reintroduced. The greater impact and social changes has come from the upgrading the A30 to a dual-carriageway, upon which the ersatz and double-decker 'ACE' now heads west.

East of Exeter, despite the longer journey times, the greatly improved service density can only be seen as a better railway for most people. This will be even better when a loop is provided at Axminster, which will increase reliability and the number of trains west of Yeovil. While I have a rose-coloured, London based view of the old Atlantic Coast Express, it is good that the Southern Way survived to provide an alternative service to London for those of us living in Exeter and around the stations in between, that were overlooked by the old named express.

1 - In later years, I could make a two-minute connection from an incoming mainline train to a suburban departure!
2 - Little did I realise this would not only add to my interest in all things railway but form the foundation for later geographical and artistic observation, and a life-long pleasure of just watching out of the window when travelling by train.
3 - Some years later, working on the same principle, when still regularly travelling on passes to Weymouth, I always booked to Jersey. I was never told that there was no connection from this train, or how to get to the harbour or even, "There is no boat today". The travelling collector population seemed not to be so vigilant or concerned about passengers' needs in the early seventies as they were in the late fifties.
4 - In 1960
5 - Sometimes the 'Merchant Navy' runs forward and immediately reverses back through the station alongside its train, drifting past with the crew happily watching the faces of the passengers.
6 - Such a collection, although not the ACE, was illustrated on page 41 of Issue 4 of 'Southern Way'. The practice of adding banking locomotives (M7) to the front of down trains is well documented. The main reason for this was to save paths across the GW mainline at the bottom of the hill, with the pilots running off quickly into the middle siding beyond Red Cow Crossing.

There's hustle and bustle and shuffling here,
There's pushing and shoving and elbowing there,
And hauling and heaving of baggage and cases,
And tipping of porters with insolent faces.
There's shouting and pouting and anticipation,
There's scurry and flurry and procrastination,
And searching for tickets and buying of papers,
From men who sell ice cream and chocolate wafers.

Shivering, sweltering mass of humanity,
Faces perplexed or of utter inanity,
Dodging and jostling their way to the barrier,
Giving no way to the old or the tarrier.

Hurrying, scurrying, bright lights and kissing,
Then to the platform where engines are hissing,
Jumping and waving and slamming and banging,
And stilted goodbyes or else cheerful haranguing.
Then at the whistle amid the commotion,
The train heaves a sigh and jerks into motion,
It trundles on happily, way out of sight,
Leaving the station alone with the night.

Jane Dean

(A definite 'first for 'SW', a husband and wife as separate contributors. See Martin Dean's recollections on page 95).

Photograph 'near Waterloo' - Howard Butler collection.

'REBUILDING'-THE LETTERS AND COMMENTS PAGE(S)

As referred to in the introduction, no doubt the increasing frequency of 'SW' is generating more (welcome) comment, starting this time with a reasoned discourse from Alastair Wilson. "I would suggest that that most evocative photograph of the concourse at Waterloo (*SW No. 7*, p. 2.) can be dated rather more accurately than the "late Southern / early BR" which is suggested. The clues are in the clothing:

1. The lady immediately behind the Police sergeant is wearing a transparent plastic raincoat: they didn't appear over here – or were certainly not on sale generally - until the very late 1950s.

2. Although, given the English weather, this is not conclusive, people are wearing winter/spring/autumn clothing, suggesting a date from October through to the following April. If this is correct, then, if the date was pre-1956, the sailor would have been wearing a blue hat, not the white-topped one.

3. At least half the men visible are hatless / capless: if the date were at the end of the '40s, it may be suggested that they would all have worn hats or caps.

4. The hair-style of the young lady in the foreground seems to me to be more late '50s than '40s (date, I hasten to add, not age), and my wife (then wife-to-be) had a

similar style of coat in 1957.

All this suggests to me a date in the late 1950s: the time is around the middle of the day – the departure time of the first train on the indicator seems to be 12-something. Is this a Saturday crowd, going home after a Saturday morning's work? And, despite the fact that most seem to be wearing raincoats of one sort or another, there's not an umbrella in sight, rolled or otherwise. This suggests that it was not actually raining: therefore people were wearing a heavy-ish raincoat as a general-purpose winter coat, reinforcing the suggestion that the date is October-April, rather than a rainy summer's day, which in turn confirms that the year is post -1956, given the sailor's white hat.

The only possible contra-indication to support the late -'40s date is the header to the poster board, immediately to the left of No. 6 platform gate, which is still headed 'SOUTHERN'. But – and I'm sure there is someone out there who will know – were they ever changed, before the platform-end barriers were altered?"

Next Peter Squibb, who contributed the delightful 'Southern Exposure' to Issue 7 writes as follows concerning the rear cover of Issue 7. "The photo on the back cover is Christ's Hospital "A". We had a happy week there removing the frame etc after a mysterious but very convenient fire had wrecked the place. The box was put out of use and the arms removed from the signals but one up train stood at the signal illustrated waiting for it to be pulled off!!" (We have asked Peter to consider a further written piece for a future issue of 'SW').

My photo editing is quite correctly taken to task now by Viv Orchard. "Kevin, another good edition, thanks. No doubt dozens have mentioned an error on pp 98 & 99. Top picture p99 refers to signal at Tadworth. It is not there! It is in picture on p98. Further the line and signal are NOT ex LB&SCR but SE&CR. The post is slotted concrete ex SE&CR. Slotted for lightness. Viv.

Now a wonderful addition to Les Duffel's picture of the 5BEL set passing Liphook, again Issue 7. "My guess would be that Les Duffel's picture of the unit

passing through Liphook was taken on 14th April 1952, when unit 3052 took the young Prince Charles and Princess Anne from Waterloo to Portsmouth to board the newly-commissioned Royal Yacht 'Britannia' for a voyage to Tobruk to be reunited with their parents who were returning from a three-month tour of Australia. According to Julian Morel, then a senior officer of the Pullman Car Company, Prince Charles was surprised by the absence of a locomotive and enquired whether there was a man at the front. During the journey he and Princess Anne were taken through the train to meet the motorman.

The headcode (07), indicates a non-stop run from Waterloo to Portsmouth & Southsea which was presumably a more convenient location than the

As mention is Issue 7, just as we were going to press with that issue, a extra view of the signalling school at Clapham Junction arrived. Rather than the perhaps bland but clinical 'official' type views previously seen, this one has what would certainly be more of a focus on human-interest. Not surprising as it is from the Corbis Press collection. We also see a bit more detail of the actual operation of the railway. The gentleman in railway uniform is presumably controlling matters, (powering the various tracks?) with the suited man (another instructor?) driving the trains. One student is operating the frame whilst the others observe. (Despite receiving, with grateful thanks, reminiscences from several loco men, we have still not had much from signalmen or anyone who was trained here at Clapham. Contributions welcome........ .)

Corbis HU021969

Harbour station if 'Britannia' was berthed in the naval dockyard. (With grateful thanks to Stephen Grant).

Keith Muston of the South Western Circle also kindly forwarded a letter he had received from Circle member Tony Wright. We have written to Tony to thank him for his contribution. "The photograph on page 4 of Southern Way 6 taken at Swanwick station on the line from Fareham to St Denys was very likely taken at about this time of the year sometime early in the first part of the 20th Century.

"Normally Swanwick would have had no more than 3-4 staff and would have been under the control of the Station Master at Fareham. This appears to be a photograph of staff brought in from all stations between Fareham and Southampton to cope with the loading of all the extra trains needed to distribute all the soft fruit grown in what was the largest area of soft fruit cultivation in the UK in those days. Several trains extra left Swanwick and Fareham every afternoon for 4-6 weeks for various parts of the country and therefore many extra staff were needed as well as the growers own personnel to load these trains. Also from early morning there would be trains of empties arriving back at these stations to be got ready for the afternoon and evening.

"Some of these trains were heading as far north as Edinburgh and Glasgow as well as the north of England towns and cities. My grandfather always looked forward to this time of the year as it meant plenty of overtime taking his trains as far as Oxford via Basingstoke and Reading or maybe further still via the Didcot, Newbury and Southampton line and of course the short runs to London (Covent Garden)."

I am now taken to task by Laurie Mack for which I apologise not only to Laurie but also to 'SW' readers. It is appropriate also that Mr Mack's comments are reproduced in full. "Dear Mr Robertson, As founder of the Southern Carriage and Wagon Society in 1960, and compiler of all its data sheets and news sheets (which means I own the copyright!) I have over the years been in touch with a few of the 100 or so members, and we are still adding to the research work which a small number of us did over about seven years; we laid the foundations for much of what has been published since, including Mike King's authoritative work on Maunsell loco-hauled coaches. I was thus intrigued to see that *SONS* data sheets SL13 and SL17 had survived in Roger Merry-Price's files to emerge in SW7.

"Unfortunately, somewhere in drafting or editing, the universal convention that a text or list is continued forwards from one page to the next and is not broken up into bits jumping backwards and forwards between pages, seems to have been lost sight of. I would guess that someone photocopied SL17/1 and SL17/2, pasted the bits together and did not ask "why was there a page break?" The result is that the Horsted (mis-spelled with an "a" throughout the article) Keynes collection is not listed in the standing order in which SL17 was painstakingly drawn

up and which the article claims that it follows.

"Can we therefore have a correcting note in SW8, please, explaining that in the Horsted Keynes standing order, 7409 - 3717 follow 809; 3664-3206 follow 3717; and 3671-3740 follow 3206 (thus, 5155 follows 5591 and 3752 follows 814).

"There is also an erroneous caption to S7797S on p88; it reads "All these vehicles later ran as open seconds, witness the sealed doorways." Disregarding the non-sequitur, they did not run later at all, of course; they were condemned, and went to the scrap yard. The reference to running as open seconds should read "These vehicles ran as open seconds from 1956 until their withdrawal: the unclassified opens were built with doors to alternate bays only, but provided with droplights to every bay - reflecting Maunsell's corridor side practice.

"In Terry Cole's Rolling Stock File, p98, is yet another error; it is claimed that the alphabetic code "was used on the all the rebuilt sets."... ....oh dear, no, it was not! It is common knowledge that the South London, Wimbledon - West Croydon and 2NOL units (1801-90, everyone of them a rebuild) always carried numeric headcodes. Having sorted that out, carry on digging out those rare photos! Yours sincerely......."

We are always pleased to receive more from Eric Youldon, this time concerning livery details. "At the beginning of 1949, a decision was taken to drop the wording BRITISH RAILWAYS on repainted locomotives, the argument being that they couldn't belong to anyone else. So until about eight months later, when the lion-and-wheel crest transfers became available, tanks and tenders of repainted engines were left blank. In the case of 32421 on page 55 (Issue 7), the Atlantic was ex-works on 15/5/49 hence the plain tender. It received the BR crest when it was next repainted, ex-works date 9/11/51. J1 32325 on page 59 is another blank example.

" With reference to the details on page 38 of the Mixed Traffic Exchanges in 1948 on the WR, these took place between Bristol and Plymouth, not as stated. On the same page you correctly quote 7/6/45 as the date when 35019 (as 21C19) entered service, but its naming ceremony date should be shown as held on 22/9/45 in Southampton Docks when the name read 'French Line CGT'.

"Page 94 etc. Thanks for publishing my comments but you have misprinted 'common' for 'uncommon' against the Exeter central photograph which unfortunately reverses the meaning about the drifting steam. On page 97 my 110 Light Pacifics has shrunk to 100".

Last but certainly by no means least. In the piece with the wonderful views of the damaged 'River' class loco following the Sevenoaks derailment, Issue 7 again, I have committed the cardinal sin. The photographs were kindly submitted by Mike Rhodes. The use of an incorrect surname in the acknowledgements was a regrettable error.

Permanent Way Notes by Graham Hatton

Formation Renewal at Paddock Wood

The article in the last issue of 'Southern Way' looked at mechanised ballast-cleaning. This mechanism is suitable for dirty ballast where the old ballast does not contain clay in any quantity. A ballast cleaner may break clay into lumps not dissimilar from stone if it is dry and simply return this to the track where it offers very poor support and drainage properties causing early failure of the 'renewed' ballast. If the clay is wet and sticky the cleaner soon gets clogged with this material sticking to the chains and screens, and ballast-cleaning is then usually curtailed. For a ballast-cleaner to be successful the formation being addressed must contain ballast, dust derived from stone or material containing no clay or at worse, very small amounts of hard clay. Of course, the treatment for the ballast will have been worked out in advance with trial holes being opened out to look and confirm the underlying situation. Inevitably, however, sometimes more extensive clay will appear unexpectedly. The ballast condition is now subject to extensive testing prior to the work, but back in the 1940s this was largely limited to a few trial holes with very extensive use being made of 'local knowledge' and visible signs of ballast contamination.

When clay is expected to be a significant issue then 'digging' the formation becomes the alternative ballast treatment to remove as much of the offending poor formation as practical. Of course you cannot dig to any great depths to remove all the clay, but typically the engineer would require a finished ballast formation for the track of a minimum of nine inches of clean ballast. So if the clay - and normally in the Southern area this was London clay - or its derivatives extended beyond this in depth, some form of 'blanketing' or 'blinding' of the remaining clay with a layer of sand or dust would take place to stop, as far as possible, the migration of the very small clay particles up through the ballast to the surface. These give

the characteristic white clay areas visible in 'failed' ballast which are still seen today. This additional layer required at least a further three inches of depth to the formation to be dug out. The term 'ballast failure' reflects the fact that when this stage is reached the ballast, which normally provides good drainage, track support and lateral restraint from track displacement, now cannot offer any of these and will lead to rough rides, track twists and ultimately vehicle derailments.

Small areas can be dealt with manually by digging the affected ballast out and replacing with new, although any actual blanketing is not normally associated with small areas. However it is not unusual to get long lengths badly affected by clay infiltration and poor drainage (normally blocked by the same clay reduced to a slurry and then settling out in the pipes). The impaired integrity of the track to support trains at particularly, but not exclusively, high speed then requires the imposition of a speed restriction.

Large scale track renewals were still in their infancy at the time of the Second World War. Renewals took place, but were largely manual, requiring significant sized work forces to complete. The work usually entailed 'opening out the ballast' to the bottom of the existing sleepers, re-sleepering the track and then adding new or semi clean ballast back before manually lifting the track to line and level.

After the Second World War several factors affecting the railway had changed. Train speeds and particularly weights had increased, mechanised plant, albeit primitive by today's standards had become available largely through war developments, manpower was reduced and more expensive, in addition to which in many cases little had been done below the sleepers since the railway was built.

When the original lines were built, formation at the base layer unable to support the new railway would have been seen. The companies adopted various means of addressing this issue as it was also long before the present day of modern geotextile material currently used to separate and strengthen materials in poor areas.

Commonly, large stones, often referred to as 'pitching stones' were used in the formation base, though sometimes various rafts or matting were used to spread the load on poor formations and give a more even loading per square inch. Where pitching stones were found in Southern days or more recently, they are left undisturbed. They rarely give trouble on their own and still act as a good base as they were always intended to do! Removing them often makes the situation less stable

The views accompanying this article were taken in 1947 at Paddock Wood on the Kent coast mainline and at

Clapham Junction, though the process and machinery in use are very similar in both locations.

Photo 1 - opposite page; This picture is on the latter site and even without benefit of colour, the dirty ballast can be seen to be lumpy and contain the offending clay. The face shovel on the excavator is digging the material and will have loaded it to wagons to be unceremoniously dumped in a suitable railway landfill site, often an old quarry such as Godstone on the Redhill to Tonbridge line, as used by the Southern Railway. Wellington boots would be an essential item in this sort of work, whilst the picture simply contains the ominous words 'blanketing clay' on the reverse! The depth of dig here and in the following pictures is the item to note. It was slow work with this machinery and produced a lot of material. Small portions totalling just a few track lengths would generally be the normal amount tackled. The drainage pipe may well have been dug up as well, though if it was possible to reuse the clay pipes in use at this time, then they would be rodded and cleaned in situ during or prior to the work, any breakages being repaired. Water ingress into the pipes was at the loose joints; more recent pipes have slits in them.

Photo 2 - above; This was taken on the Down Main at Paddock Wood. It gives a good idea of the depth and hence

quantity of material removed to get rid of the contaminated ballast. This is a large site for blanketing. The single wagon is slightly misleading; there are usually several trains of open wagons to take away the spoil from the site! It is not clear in the view why just a single wagon was positioned at this point.

Sometimes a few wagons were left coupled in spaced out blocks and the excavators would nudge them along. This was very unofficial, but life was less regimented then!

Getting the machine to site would have been a challenge, some were transferred on low well-wagons, and some would just be moved over sleepered-out neighbouring tracks. Any conductor rail would just be lowered by removing the conductor rail pots, but at this stage, 1947, Paddock Wood was still a non-electrified area.

Of note also in the photo is the elevated signalbox, a characteristic of this station for many years. There were (and still are) similar boxes elsewhere where restricted sites demanded building across, as at Canterbury West, cantilevering out from a narrow base and Canterbury East (both of which remain in use), and over a single track as here. These boxes made operation easier but tended to require extra cranks to be used to get the rodding down and along the track which needed careful setting up to avoid 'binding' in the rod runs. The type of lever frame in use meant the locking mechanism was contained in the room below the operational floor, so the box was of considerable height. Note also the co-acting Down signals and stays. These signals required servicing by staff with steady nerves. If a train passed below you could be in the smoke swaying around quite a bit!

The style of platform wall and platform surface tended to present long term problems as the walls migrated towards the adjacent track sometimes with the fill pushing from behind. The surface is very different from the smooth type now in more general use at most stations.

Photo 3 - this page;

Having dug to the correct depth (checked by technical staff with levels and gauges), the material being unloaded here is the base blanketing or blinding sand. Sand was usually used, but Meldon dust (a derivative from the granite ballast quarried there), was an alternative and when compacted gave a very hard base layer which was also used for pathways. There is no machinery here, you got in the wagon with your mate and shovelled out the material through the dropped side door. It was slow hard work and very dirty to boot! The Engineers tended to use any available open wagon as seen in this picture. Specific engineer's wagons (company opens) were also available for this work. The discharged sand / dust would then be spread by hand or with some form of dozer. The face shovel would be no use for this as it is a loading implement.

If a cross fall on the formation did not already exist towards the drain it would be installed to 'encourage'

the water to flow in the right direction.

The dense layer of sand / dust would, to a large degree, stop the very small clay particles from migrating up through the new ballast and clogging it.

Clean ballast would then be unloaded on the levelled sand or dust to the level of the underside of the sleepers, which would then be replaced. Re-railing followed and finally top ballast would be added.

Usually with dig jobs the original ballast would not be reused, however sometimes the better ballast (usually the top ballast), would be thrown out on the other track for reuse.

Work in the following week would be to manually lift and pack the track to maintain the top level and as the ballast compacted under traffic. No real compactors were available so you could expect in time typically two inches of track settlement and compaction of ballast. As a result of this, the track would often initially appear over ballasted initially to allow sufficient ballast for topping up and hand packing.

The principles of this work have changed little over the years. Modern machinery has replaced the early digger and it is usually the ubiquitous road / rail machine.

Modern geotextile material, a filtering tough woven material, helps to prevent the clay moving upwards through the clean ballast. The layers of material fill are compacted by modern vibrating rollers or 'wacker' plates, lasers guide the technical staff in getting levels 'spot on', and tampers thoroughly lift, line and compact the ballast previously done by hand, but the underlying process is still the same.

MEMORIES OF

TUNBRIDGE WELLS WEST

Martin Dean

It is difficult to image the genteel town of Tunbridge Wells being the centre of a battle zone. However, that is what it became in the 19th century as the South Eastern Railway (SER) attempted to use the town as a base from which to penetrate into Sussex whilst the London Brighton & South Coast Railway (LBSCR) used it as a defensive bastion determined to keep it out. The result was that the Brighton built a network of lines in Sussex serving the surrounding small towns and villages as well as linking to the main traffic centres – London and Brighton. All these routes had their focal point in Tunbridge Wells.

However, the first railway to reach Tunbridge Wells was the SER branch from Tonbridge which opened in 1846. The station in Mount Pleasant was originally on the outskirts of town but gradual urban expansion meant that it became increasingly in the centre. The site was cramped and when the line was extended towards Hastings the station found itself built on a curve and squeezed between two tunnels. Although eventually having the benefit of a central location the architecture was dictated by the limited space available. Nevertheless a modest clock tower was incorporated into the design.

The LBSCR fully recognised the threat to its territory from the SER and slowly began to extend its own lines to stop any possible invasion. Its first line was from Three Bridges and East Grinstead and this opened for business on 1st October 1866 as did its station in Tunbridge Wells. A direct link from Brighton via Uckfield followed nearly two years later in 1868. Further lines opened to Eastbourne via Heathfield in 1880 and to Oxted in 1888, the latter providing a direct and competing service to London. On the eastern side of the station a single line link to the SER was opened in 1867 through Grove Tunnel.

To meet the needs of these services and to make a clear statement that it had truly 'arrived', the LBSCR built an imposing station in a select, if quiet, part of town. It was designed to impress and outperform the SER station in every way; that it certainly did. In addition, the fact that it was located just over the county border in Kent was surely not lost on the SER. The station's proud and dignified Victorian architecture reflected the immediate area's rising status as a desirable residential part of town. Although designed as a terminus, the single line through Grove Tunnel forced a rethink. Consequently it was finally built as a through station although initially there was very little through traffic to the SER.

It is thought that the station was designed by the Brighton's Chief Engineer, F. Dale Bannister. It has been described as 'The St. Pancras of the Weald'. Largely built of red brick with limestone and black brick dressings, the whole is dominated by a three storey clock tower. It has a pyramid-shaped slate roof topped by an ornamental cupola complete with weather vane. The main station building is of two-storey height with similar black brick and limestone decoration. At one time there were five platform faces; three through lines and two bays. An island platform built in complementary style to the main structure was linked to the main platform by an underground passageway. In Brighton days the station was known simply as Tunbridge Wells it being felt unnecessary to recognise that there was another establishment in the town. However, the newly formed Southern Railway clearly recognised the opportunity for confusion and added the suffix 'West' in August 1923 whilst the SER station was called 'Central'. Both titles accurately reflected the positions of the stations in the town.

It was during a series of regular visits to Tunbridge Wells in the mid / late 1970s that I first came upon the station. By this time the Central station had been given the Corporate Image makeover with twin arrowed logo etc. I followed the discreet finger posts pointing the way to the West station, all complete with corporate logo. They certainly did not prepare me for my destination.

The approach to Tunbridge Wells West station was up a quiet tree-lined Victorian road. There was no traffic. The station building which faced me was large and imposing and on the cobbles outside the main entrance a lone Ford Cortina was parked. The whole silent scene was dominated by the majestic clock tower whose clock had long since ceased to function and whose weather vane was fixed, presumably rusted into place by countless rain storms. The building was unkempt; gutters were blocked or broken and rough weeds sprouted from the flagstones on the pavement. It was a sad sight.

Yet the station was open for business. No corporate signs here, for on the clock tower was a large green totem with the proud wording 'SOUTHERN'. The station was painted in dark green and cream although much of the paint was peeling. There was broken timber and the obvious signs of neglect were everywhere to be seen. A building of such dignity and quality did not deserve this treatment.

I approached the green station doors with a sense of trepidation for I felt that I was about to trespass and enter where I should not. Under the long front canopy the station doors had been protected from the ravages of the weather. They were almost smart, yet this was only a prelude. The booking office was a complete step back in time. The floor was bare boards; only a sprinkling of water kept the dust in check. Tall sash windows gave plenty of light into a room with a high ceiling. From the centre of ornate roses long pipes descended, each connected to a hissing gas lamp. Every lamp was lit even though natural light flooded the scene. The tall stone columns which supported the structure had been painted dark green as was the bottom half of the partition wall that separated the passengers from the ticket office staff. Needless to say the ticket office was closed and I believe that at the time of my visits Tunbridge Wells West was unstaffed. This was hardly a deserving fate for such a magnificent station.

If the booking office was awe inspiring, it little prepared me for the main platform. Southern Railway green enamelled signs proliferated under the main canopy pointing the way to waiting room, toilets etc. The platform number was pure Southern Railway whilst Southern Region green totems indicated the location. Again, all were lit by the hissing green-enamelled gas lamps so beloved of the Southern. The platform canopy was showing severe signs of neglect for at the eastern end of the platform it was supported by rough wooden staging. I tested the 'gents' and found them to be fully operational in spite of the fact that the building was showing signs of damage and decay. They were wonderful; no modern moulded porcelain here for the facilities still retained the heavy slate partitioned urinal cubicles so beloved of the Victorians. Total privacy was guaranteed!

The station buildings on the island platform had been razed to the ground. Where the underground subway emerged a crude structure of scaffold poles with corrugated iron sheets had been erected. This at least stopped the worst of any weather flooding down the passageway. The only passenger comfort was a wooden Southern Railway waiting room seat. Designed for interior use, it was totally unsuited for its new life in a semi-open location. It was rough, uneven and had certainly seen better days.

Although goods traffic had long since ceased, the goods yard was still largely intact although much of it was used as a DMU stabling point. The original Brighton goods shed was still standing as was the locomotive shed (once 75F). The latter was in a sorry state of repair with many broken windows and cracked asbestos sheeting forming the roof. The track had gone and the site seemed ready for demolition. However, Tunbridge Wells West was still fully signalled with two signal cabins, one at each end of the station. A gantry at the western end controlled the limited traffic in that direction whilst the single line token apparatus was housed in the cabin protecting the line to Central through Grove Tunnel.

The 1950s saw Tunbridge Wells West's heyday with over 130 passenger train movements. On average a passenger train arrived or departed every 8 minutes between 06.00 and midnight. Trains to a variety of destinations using six routes served the station. However, by the time of my visits an hourly service between Tonbridge and Eridge (with a connection to Uckfield) was all that remained. Passenger traffic was almost non existent. I well remember standing on the bleak island platform having ventured from the corrugated iron shelter and seeing a young woman with a baby in her arms as the only people waiting to catch the 14.12 to Groombridge and Eridge. Yet even in this seemingly forgotten outpost, the Corporate Image could not be forgotten. On the main platform under the canopy the posters on the Southern Railway notice boards beamed with the face of Jimmy Saville reminding us that this was the 'Age of the Train'. Strangely, it didn't feel like it.

The station's silence was overwhelming. This, coupled with the Victorian splendour of the main structure made one feel that the ghosts of the past were everywhere. From the cobbles outside where hansom cabs once stood to the atmospheric booking office where all and sundry queued for their tickets it was easy to capture the spirit of past years. Possibly it was the hissing of the gas lamps. Whenever I returned they were still working and I believe that Tunbridge Wells West retained them to the end of its operational railway life. I understand it was the last station on British Rail to retain this form of lighting.

The station closed to all traffic in July 1985 and the track was lifted. Today the site has changed forever with its peace and tranquillity destroyed. The goods yard with its original LBSCR shed has been levelled and the area is now occupied by Sainsburys and Homebase. The locomotive shed, which I had largely written off at the time of my visits, has been restored and is now the home of The Spa Valley Railway. This runs to Groombridge and hopes one day to reach Eridge where a connection could be made with the National rail network. The main station building remains largely intact being used as a pub/restaurant. An extension has been built under the canopy where the green enamelled signs once proliferated. In 1986, a year after passenger traffic ceased, the main station building was given Grade 2 Listed Building status. This belated recognition by English Heritage of the significance of the station's architectural importance certainly stopped any demolition threat.

I now have no need to visit Tunbridge Wells but I will always treasure my memories of a largely forgotten station that was quietly and gently fading away. My only regret is that I did not discover this gem when its services were at their height. I really should have used my Dad's 'priv' tickets more often!

Page 97 - The hissing gas lamps illuminate the empty ticket office at Tunbridge Wells West. The ornate architectural detail at the top of the columns and above the interior windows of the partition separating the public and the staff areas all point to the fact that this was a building designed to impress. Unfortunately, the modern signs and leaflet rack intrude into the largely unspoilt Victorian scene.

Left - The silent clock tower dominates an equally silent Tunbridge Wells West. This view looks towards Groombridge and shows the original LBSCR goods shed, the West signal cabin and the signal gantry controlling all movements in that direction. The platforms, complete with their impressive array of green totems, have received the benefit of electric lighting although the station and the area under the canopy are still lit by gas. The station building on the island platform has gone, replaced by a crude corrugated iron shelter whilst the cross over in the foreground was taken out of use when terminating steam-hauled services ceased.

Above - Only the double yellow lines on the roadway give a clue that this picture was taken some 25 years after nationalisation. This Southern Railway scene is complete with the Exmouth Junction concrete lamp post to the left and imposing station enamel sign. This simple LBSCR station located in a quiet street was designed to serve a relatively small community. However, the expansion of London in the inter-war years changed that forever.

Overleaf - The end of the line at the end of its days. Plymouth Friary is seen some 15 years after passenger traffic ceased in 1958. The station had become the city's main goods depot but by the time this picture was taken the station area was used as a freight concentration depot, hence the number of guard's vans. The deterioration of the station is quite obvious and gives a good indication of how quickly stations not in public use can fall into disrepair.

Issue No 9 of *THE SOUTHERN WAY* (ISBN 978-1-906419-28-8) should be available in January 2010

At the time of going to press we are hoping to include features on the C2 / C2X classes by Gerry Bixley, a further instalment on LANCING CARRIAGE WORKS, Part 3 of BASINGSTOKE etc etc - plus our usual features.

To receive your copy the moment it is released, order in advance from your usual supplier, or direct from the publisher:

Kevin Robertson (Noodle Books) PO Box 279, Corhampton, SOUTHAMPTON, SO32 3ZX

Tel / Fax 01489 877880

www.kevinrobertsonbooks.co.uk

We are also working on a further 'Southern Way Special ' for 2010

This is planned for late Spring 2010. Further details will be announced as soon as possible..